The Best
Stage Scenes
of 2004

D1565659

Smith and Kraus *Books for Actors*
YOUNG ACTOR SERIES
Great Scenes and Monologues for Children Volumes I and II

Forensics Series Volume I: Duo Practice and Competition: Thirty-five
8–10 Minute Original Comedic Plays

Forensics Series Volume II: Duo Practice and Competition: Thirty-five
8–10 Minute Original Dramatic Plays

Great Scenes in Dialect for Young Actors Volumes I and II

Great Scenes for Young Actors Volumes I and II

Short Scenes and Monologues for Middle School Actors

Multicultural Scenes for Young Actors

SCENE STUDY SERIES
The Best Stage Scenes of 2003

The Best Stage Scenes of 2002

The Best Stage Scenes of 2001

The Best Stage Scenes of 2000

The Best Stage Scenes of 1999

The Best Stage Scenes of 1998

The Best Stage Scenes of 1997

The Best Stage Scenes of 1996

The Best Stage Scenes of 1995

The Best Stage Scenes of 1994

The Best Stage Scenes of 1993

The Best Stage Scenes of 1992

The Best Stage Scenes for Men from the 1980s

The Best Stage Scenes for Women from the 1980s

The Ultimate Scene Study Series Volume I: 101 Short Scenes for Groups

The Ultimate Scene Study Series Volume II: 102 Short Scenes for Two Actors

The Ultimate Scene Study Series Volume III: 103 Short Scenes for Three Actors

The Ultimate Scene Study Series Volume IV: 104 Short Scenes for Four Actors

Kiss and Tell—Restoration Comedy of Manners: Scenes, Monologues, and
Historical Context

A Brave and Violent Theatre Monologues, Scenes and Historical Context for
20th Century Irish Drama

Scenes from Classic Plays 468 BC to 1970 AD

If you require prepublication information about upcoming Smith and Kraus books, you may receive our semiannual catalogue, free of charge, by sending your name and address to *Smith and Kraus Catalogue, PO Box 127, Lyme, NH 03768. Or call us at (800) 895-4331; fax: (603) 643-6431.*

The Best
Stage Scenes
of 2004

edited by D. L. Lepidus

SCENE STUDY SERIES

A SMITH AND KRAUS BOOK

Published by Smith and Kraus, Inc.
177 Lyme Road, Hanover, NH 03755
www.SmithKraus.com

First Edition: August 2004
10 9 8 7 6 5 4 3 2 1

Cover illustration by Lisa Goldfinger
Cover and text design by Julia Hill Gignoux

The Scene Study Series 1067-3253
ISBN 1-57525-404-2

NOTE: These scenes are intended to be used for audition and class study; permission is not required to use the material for those purposes. However, if there is a paid performance of any of the scenes included in this book, please refer to the Rights and Permissions pages 219–224 to locate the source that can grant permission for public performance.

Contents

Scenes for Two Women

Foreword

I have been privileged to edit Smith and Kraus' exemplary annual series of scene and monologue books since 2001, so this is the fourth scene book I have done. When I agreed to take on this project, I determined to find the best scenes I could find, from the best plays I could find. Here's what I mean by "best."

I've selected scenes that are all from published or readily available plays (see the Rights and Permissions section in the back of this book for information), because I know that you have to have access to the entire text of a play if you are going to work on it in class or use it for an audition.

I've selected scenes for characters almost exclusively under forty (most, under thirty) because, in general, younger actors are the ones who need this book the most.

And these scenes are written in a wide variety of styles. Many are very dramatic (meaning not many laughs); many are comic (meaning dramatic, too, but with a lotta laughs).

Here are scenes from the work of some of our finest contemporary playwrights, writers such as Richard Greenberg, Don Nigro, Paul Rudnick, and John Patrick Shanley. But here, too, are terrific scenes from many fine "new" playwrights, such as Sunil Kuruvilla, Kirsten Greenidge, Gina Gionfriddo, Tracey Scott Wilson, Rinne Groff, and Jonathan Rand.

Here are, lastly, forty-five scenes which I sincerely hope will be of great use to you — perhaps the best definition of *good*.

D. L. Lepidus

Scenes for
One Man and
One Woman

AFTER ASHLEY
Gina Gionfriddo

Seriocomic
Justin, eighteen; Julie (maybe a little older — but not much)

> *Justin's mother, Ashley, was brutally murdered four years ago. His father has written a best-selling book about coping with his grief, and he's just been asked to host a TV talk show focusing on other survivors of terrible crimes. Justin is determined to thwart his father's efforts to exploit the murder of his mother, possibly with the help of Julie, a quasi-goth college coed he's met in a bar.*

JULIE: Wow.

JUSTIN: We don't have to have dinner. I just needed to stall him.

JULIE: We can have dinner.

JUSTIN: Do you have any thoughts on this?

JULIE: Yeah. It's completely horrible and it should be stopped. *(Pause.)* Also they've got the Joe Jackson song really, really wrong.

JUSTIN: No kidding.

JULIE: It's not about women being fragile; it's about their capacity for . . . cruelty being equal to men's, if not worse.

JUSTIN: Very good. You're smarter than I thought.

JULIE: For a C.F.U. student.

JUSTIN: I'm sorry I said that. *(Pause.)* I need advice, preferably female, and you're here and you understand Joe Jackson and on a purely gut instinct level, I like you.

JULIE: OK.

JUSTIN: So I'm gonna trust you and if it turns out I'm wrong and you really are just ambulance-chasing trash . . . If you screw me over, I will . . . I will qualify you for Ashley House and I'm not just fucking with you, I'm serious. OK?

JULIE: OK.

JUSTIN: OK. I'm gonna show you something.

(Justin gets up and rifles through some things. He returns with a manila envelope.)

JULIE: What's in there?

JUSTIN: When I found my mom . . . I called the police and when I was waiting for them, I thought . . . Before the reality of the situation set in and freaked me out I got really, um, practical. Like literally the first thing I thought was, "My mom's got all this pot in her room and I don't want her to get in trouble." Which is insane, she's dead, but . . .

JULIE: I understand.

JUSTIN: So I took her pot —

JULIE: Is that what you have in the envelope — pot?

JUSTIN: No. Please shut up and let me talk.

JULIE: Sorry.

JUSTIN: I found the pot and I took it. A lot later, I smoked it. But I also found this and I took it, too.

JULIE: What is it?

(Justin takes a clothbound book out of the envelope and hands it to Julie.)

JULIE: What is it — a journal?

JUSTIN: Read the pages with the sticky notes.

(Julie starts to read.)

JULIE: I don't think I should read this.

JUSTIN: What's your problem?

JULIE: It's . . . really personal.

JUSTIN: Fine. Skip a couple months.

(Justin flips pages to another marked section. Julie reads more.)

JULIE: OK. I get the idea.

JUSTIN: What is wrong with you?

JULIE: It's really upsetting, Justin.

JUSTIN: Why? Because she had sex . . . orgies with strangers?

JULIE: No. I'm not judgmental about stuff like that.

JUSTIN: Is it because they filmed them?

JULIE: No. None of that stuff is . . . bad in and of itself. It just doesn't sound like she liked it. I don't know. Doing sexual stuff you don't want to do makes me really upset. It might be a girl thing.

JUSTIN: The re-enactments didn't bother you.

JULIE: Right. You're right. Score one, Justin. You made your point.

JUSTIN: Well. It's my fault she . . . did it, so . . . I just wanted to know.

JULIE: How is it your fault?

JUSTIN: I told her to read the *City Paper*. I told her to go to a poetry reading or something and she found this . . . sex cult . . . thing.

JULIE: In the sex ads?

JUSTIN: I guess.

JULIE: She made the choice. To go and go back. *(Pause.)* It's not a terrible thing. It's a sad thing, but . . . I mean, it's not like this had anything to do with . . . you know. Did it?

(Pause.)

JUSTIN: She was really unhappy and . . . bitchy. That's why I told her to go do something, but after she went she got worse. Not to me, but . . . You know. To Dad or . . . whoever happened to be there. She could just cut a person down . . .

JULIE: Are you saying she mouthed off to . . . the guy? To him?

JUSTIN: That day, I don't know. Other times, yeah.

(Pause.)

JULIE: You're not the person who brought him home you know?

JUSTIN: Yeah, but I also didn't stop it.

JULIE: Neither did she.

(Pause.)

JUSTIN: Before the shelter thing, my dad had a plan to put up a statue in some kiddie park in DC. It was gonna be mom feeding the birds which is insane . . . She liked birds like she liked kids which is not at all. Anyway, he got the TV show and he blew off the statue, but I had this idea of how to stop it if I had to. *(Pause.)* I was gonna call this guy Roderick and get the videos.

JULIE: Do you know how to contact him?

JUSTIN: His number is in the journal.

JULIE: It might have changed by now.

JUSTIN: As of six months ago, it hadn't.

(Pause.)

JULIE: You would show people those tapes?

(Pause.)

JUSTIN: Yeah, I would. If it would keep her from being . . . the patron s t of battered women or the Earth Mother with the birdseed, yeah. I would. I would rather people know her for . . . herself than for someone else's totally false idea of who she is. Does that make sense?

JULIE: You really think your mom having freaky group sex would bring down Ashley House?

JUSTIN: What do you think?

(Pause.)

JULIE: Yeah, you're right. It would.

JUSTIN: She lost her life and they're trying to take her identity, too. *(Pause.)* I don't want my mother rewritten into fucking Heidi. If they do that, then . . . then she's really gone. The only way to save her is to trash her. Do you think that's crazy?

JULIE: No. I don't.

THE COMING WORLD
Christopher Shinn

Dramatic
Ed and Dora, twenties to thirties

> *Ed, struggling to make ends meet, has lost $10,000 and calls on his ex-girlfriend, Dora, for help. He also hopes to entice her back into his life. The beach. Dora approaches Ed. She startles him; he jerks.*

DORA: Ahh!

ED: Shit!

DORA: Ed!

ED: Sorry.

DORA: Jesus.

ED: Sorry. *(Ed looks at Dora, smiles.)*

DORA: (   ) *(Pause.)*

ED: *(   )*?

DORA: I don't wanna be here.

ED: I know —

DORA: I can't get in your shit now —

ED: Nothing for you to get into . . . Sit.

DORA: I'm just — if you want something (just tell me now) . . .

ED: All I want — serious — all I want is to just . . . *(   )* . . .
(She doesn't sit.) Miss you. — OK that I say that?

DORA: (You) Just did.

ED: Yeah.

DORA: You look bad.

ED: I look *bad?*

DORA: Yeah.

ED: It's dark!

DORA: What.

ED: I look bad (in the dark)?

DORA: *(Sitting.)* Circles under your eyes, unshaven . . .

ED: Really?

DORA: Are you . . . (on drugs)?

ED: No.

DORA: No?

ED: *You* look good.

DORA: I worked all day, I look tired.

ED: How was work?

DORA: (You wanna talk about) Work?

ED: What movies came in today?

DORA: They come in Tuesdays.

ED: You put them up Tuesdays, but you get them before.

DORA: (   ). *(Pause.)*

ED: (I'll) Rub your feet.

DORA: (No.)

ED: Shoulders. You look tense.

DORA: I don't (want a massage).

ED: Stressed out, standing all day, the kids, annoying, come on.

DORA: Not everyone hates their job.

ED: Thanks.

DORA: "The kids, annoying" — (actually) I like my job.

ED: Good for you. (   )?

DORA: — I'm just saying, you're making it like I hate my job.

ED: I just said do you want a massage that place stresses you out. *(Pause.)*

DORA: You have to stop calling me. *(Pause.)*

ED: Who's talking about this.

DORA: We broke up.

ED: OK.

DORA: OK?

ED: I just wanted to talk. Am I doing anything?

DORA: "Can I rub your feet."

ED: (   )?

DORA: You don't do the same thing after you break up. You don't (give
    massages) —

ED: — I don't even feel bad.

DORA: (   )?

ED: Not about you. Something else. I mean I do (feel bad) about you.

But I don't know if I (feel bad) about this other thing. Maybe after I say it I'll feel bad. — No one knows (what I did).

DORA: What are you talking/about

ED: Why do you think Ty won't talk to me?

DORA: (   ).

ED: He won't call me back. Since we hung out. Which. That was a fun night. He had fun, right?

DORA: (Like) You remember (that night).

ED: It was only a month ago.

DORA: No. Because you blacked out. (I was) Dragging you home.

ED: (You didn't) Drag me home.

DORA: Yeah (right)!

ED: He's probably just heavy into work. Computer shit. Big money. I thought it was maybe the money (he lent me) but that doesn't make sense. Why he would be mad about that.

DORA: (   )?

ED: He lent me money. I think he sent it, I think he sent it the next day, day after we hung out. We were broke up when I got the check so I didn't tell you but. In the mail. Five thousand dollars. (I was like) Shit! Five thousand dollars! Just in my mail! No note, no anything, and so — I called him, to like — I don't know, to thank him or to say (why did you send me five thousand dollars) . . . (I keep) Calling, but he won't call me back. — Why did I get so drunk that night?

DORA: He just — (sent you) five thousand dollars. *(Pause.)* (I hope) You don't need more.

ED: *(Laughs.)* Why do you say that?

DORA: Because — you don't look so good, you don't look a guy who has five thousand dollars, so — (do you need more?) . . .
(Ed reaches into his pocket, takes out ten singles.)
What (are you doing).

ED: Ten dollars.

DORA: (I know) But (why)?

ED: (This is) All I have left. *(Pause.)*

DORA: (   )?

ED: It went.

DORA: I don't (understand).

ED: Paid bills, paid — not like five's a fortune, I mean, what I owe. I was just trying to set things up, climb outta this hole —

DORA: The thousand (I gave you, is that gone too)?

ED: I paid off the credit card (with that).

DORA: Where did it (go)?

ED: . . .

DORA: I'm not (giving you anything) — Nothing.

ED: I had a job.

DORA: (   )?

ED: (I got paid a) Thousand a week.

DORA: . . .

ED: You want me to jump to the end of the story or start at the start of it?

DORA: I don't (care).

ED: It's just, I don't know which way (makes more sense) — starting and going forward or going to the end and then back. Makes sense — (not the story, but) telling you.

DORA: I'm not going to get all (wrapped up in it) . . .

ED: But do you want to hear just the outcome or how I got there . . .

DORA: It's not gonna make me *do* something (I'm not gonna do).

ED: (Do you know) I'm the only person Ty ever showed his tattoos to? I ever tell you that?

DORA: This (relates how)? . . .

ED: I'm just — trying to talk like — like there's none of this shit in between us.

DORA: (So you lost) Five thousand dollars.

ED: You think I should get a tattoo?

DORA: — They're gross.

ED: Why?

DORA: It's like self-mutilation, they're ugly.

ED: Ty showed me his. I'm the only one.

DORA: Ed. Come on.

(Ed looks at her. Pause.)

ED: OK. All right. (I'll tell you) What happened. *(Pause.)*

DORA: I don't need all kinds of details.

ED: All right. *(Pause. She turns.)* I just — there's this one question to get —

out of the way — so I can tell you what happened because, just —
I . . . *(Pause.)*

DORA: (   )?

ED: . . .

DORA: .(   )?

ED: No, I know (why you broke up with me). I had no money. What you (said), I have no (money), I'm in debt, I have no job, you can't be with someone (with) no money (and) no job . . . But — if there's (another reason) — you can tell me, I just (wanna know) —

DORA: No, there's no other reason, Ed.

ED: All right, OK, that's all I wanted (to know) . . . *(She looks out at the ocean.)* OK. OK. So. There's this (guy). I'm in the (casino) — at the least, I promise you, this is a good story.

DORA: *(Turning back to him.)* Then (start telling it).

ED: No, because you look like (you don't care) —

DORA: I'm (listening, just tell me).

ED: I'm just (saying) — . . . OK. — I haven't even told this (to anyone). OK. I'm in the casino chilling, and this guy says there's this guy he knows. And the guy, the guy I'm talking to —

DORA: (   )?

ED: (OK,) Martin.

DORA: Martin (great).

ED: Don't get all stupid.

DORA: Fucking Martin.

ED: Martin and John.

DORA: (I don't know) John (who is he)?

ED: They just know each other. John's at the casino all the time, Martin knows him from there. OK. So Martin tells me John, John needs somebody for something — under-the — quick-buck thing. Puts me in (touch) — Martin — with John — in touch so — OK? OK. So: what do I have to lose? I figure (what the hell, who knows) — so — OK. I call John. Hello, hello, come over, so. I go over. House, *his* house, oh my God. It's (fucking amazing) — totally new, mile away (from the casino) — inside — big TV, flat-screen, DVD. Guys watching *The Matrix* — the scene (where Neo fights the guy in the subway) — John sits me down, this *other* guy, guy gets *me* a drink, and I'm — (sitting) on this like electronic plush chair — massage, adjust the —

DORA: (What are all) These details . . .

ED: (Sorry, I'm getting all excited.) OK. So.OK. So John's like, a big guy, maybe thirty, well-groomed, but, like, hairy back kind of guy. (He's) Mob (and he's like —)

DORA: ?

ED: But (not scary).

DORA: Mob.

ED: (All right, but) He says, "It's a very simple thing, Ed." Simple. I'm like — (it's) like a movie, (I'm) sitting there, like — "I supply" — this is him — "I"

DORA: You don't have to get all dramatic.

ED: (You don't think it's funny?) — OK. "I supply a local man with ecstasy. He distributes it to his people at six schools. I don't like to be involved with drugs but it's a lot of money and this is as far as I go with it. It's safe, it's easy, it's very lucrative. What your job is is this:" — and I'm sitting there, with my drink, thinking like (is this really happening?) — "Your job is this:" — not would be, (but) *is* — "Once a week, you'll deliver the ecstasy to this man. You'll be paid a thousand for each delivery. All you do is come here, pick up a backpack with ten thousand dollars of pills, drive half an hour, hand it over, take the cash, bring it back, I'll cut you a thousand, and you'll go home." *(Pause.)* I mean, problem solved! Before Christmas! Four thousand a month!

DORA: So you just (say yes) . . .

ED: (I know but) I think — what if he knows some other guy, more eager guy. I don't want to (lose the chance) — Martin (must know other guys but) — he thought of me first. John's like, "Martin speaks very highly of you."

DORA: Martin speaks highly of you. Which, he knows you from (what). "He's a good drinker. He sniffs coke and loses money really well."

ED: (Fuck you.)

DORA: (   ).

ED: (   ).

DORA: Five minutes (you know this guy) and you say yes.

ED: I thought — he needs his money — drugs need to get where they're going — (it's) simple how I fit in. John said he doesn't like his guys to do it because if you get caught it's mandatory minimum sentence, so he contracts it out to keep it out of his thing. He said no one ever got caught but it's better for him that he's not directly connected to it.

DORA: Fine, so. What (happened). *(Ed pauses, staring at Dora.)* ( )?

ED: OK. So. Next day. I get the backpack. They give me a phone number. (Of) The guy I'm handing over to. I'm supposed to go to the pay phone in the parking lot of the bank near the Burger King. I call and let it ring. I can only use that pay phone because what the guy is going to do is, is look at his Caller ID, and when he sees that pay phone number, he's gonna come meet me at the bank. That way there's no talking on any phones. So. I get the backpack. I get in my car and go. Get to the Burger King, the bank, pull in, pull around back . . .

DORA: (Wait,) What time is it?

ED: What?

DORA: Is it dark? *(Short pause.)* This is the phone, the one behind the bank, out of sight of the road?

ED: There's — the Burger King —

DORA: There's the fence between the bank and the Burger King. And it's dark. (Do you see?)

ED: What are you (saying)?

DORA: (You're sitting where) No one can see you.

ED: Why would you want anyone to see?

DORA: (It's a) Backpack — you could hand it over *in* the Burger/King!

ED: You wanna tell the story? You know what happens?

DORA: ( ). *(Pause.)*

ED: (So I) Pick up the phone. Dial. Ringing. Then (I hear) a tap on the glass. (Out of) Nowhere. (I) Look. (It's a) Gun. Passenger side, guy with a gun, tapping on the glass. (I) Turn around, (my) window's rolled down, (I) still have the phone to my ear, sitting in the car, so my window is down, (I) turn. Another guy. (Guy) *Rips* the phone from my hand, hangs it up, slams it . . . (I) Give him the (backpack) . . . They just (go) . . . *(Pause. Dora looks away.)* So.

DORA: Do you know what happened?

ED: *(Grabbing stomach.)* Fuck, my stomach. Can you hear that?

DORA: What?

ED: I guess only I can hear it, 'cuz of the vibrations in my body.

DORA: What are you talking about?

ED: My stomach is making weird noises, it hurts.

DORA: — Ed, they didn't see the Caller ID, so how did they know what time you were gonna be there?

ED: I guess — I figure John probably told them around when to expect me. So they were probably just hanging out, waiting. Waiting for a car to pull in there, pick up the phone. Boom.

DORA: But . . . you don't see?

ED: (   )?

DORA: OK. So — Martin and John know each other a little, they bull-shit, whatever. One night John says to Martin, "Hey Martin, I need a favor." Martin's flattered, (he's a) bartender, (and a) mob guy needs his help. (He) Says, "Want you to find me some kid, some fuckup who needs some money. I'll jerk him around, scare him a little, but I won't hurt him, you have my word. You know anybody? (You.) Now, John's got this all planned out already with the guy — the dis-tributor guy, the dealer. John fills him in, the dealer gives him nine thousand bucks. The *dealer* gets to save a thousand, and now John has an errand boy who thinks he owes him ten thousand bucks. Who'll do whatever he wants.

ED: What . . . ?

DORA: (They) Pumped you up, gave you a bullshit story — the whole thing was planned out. Robbing *you* works out for *both* of them, they *both* save all this money, meanwhile, *you* get a gun in your face, and now *you* think you owe a mobster ten thousand bucks. Which, if he says you do, you do. So now he'll make you work it off, doing all his dirty work or whatever.

ED: I don't . . . you think he set me up? But — no. No way. John — no, there's gotta be holes in there.

DORA: There's no holes.

ED: (   ). *(Short pause.)* Oh — oh fuck —

DORA: They're not stupid, these guys, they know what they're doing. This

dealer is gonna rob a mobster? No one robs mobsters. They have a
whole system, this whole thing together, and this guy's just gonna
up and rob him? It's where he gets the ecstasy from — like you said,
they both need each other.

ED: Oh God. *(Pause.)*

DORA: (Tell me the truth,) Are you doing coke?

ED: Not — really, I don't know, a couple of times —

DORA: Five thousand dollars partying.

ED: I haven't (been partying that much), I've been paying (off my debts.) —
you doing coke?

DORA: (We're) Talking about me now?

ED: Don't be so angry.

DORA: Fine, (let's) talk about me, what do *you* want *me* to do? *(Pause.)*

ED: ( ).

DORA: So I can just leave now.

ED: All right. This is what I came up with. I thought — I can move home,
(that) kills my rent, (that) kills my bills. I gotta pay John, God knows
what he's gonna make me do to pay it off. So, get the ten thousand
out of the way, hold off my other debts —

DORA: So, what, this ten thousand is just gonna wash up on shore?

ED: Well — I gotta find a job. Obviously.

DORA: How do I fit into this.

ED: Well . . . I know I can't — stay with you.

DORA: You already figured that out, you're gonna stay with your folks.

ED: Right. *(Pause.)* I know . . . you don't have any money I could . . .
( ) . . .

DORA: ( ).

ED: I know.

DORA: So all that's left that I can do for you is fuck you, basically.

ED: (Seriously)?

DORA: ( )!

ED: Kidding Dora! I'm not (that dumb). But what's going on with you,
you seeing anybody?

DORA: ( ).

ED: I hope he's good to you, that's all I hope.

DORA: (I) Got it.

ED: What?

DORA: Ask Ty for more money.

ED: No.

DORA: Why not?

ED: That's not right.

DORA: Why not?

ED: No!

DORA: He gave you five thousand.

ED: I didn't ask for it. He just gave it to me.

DORA: So?

ED: What I don't understand is. Because you said you love me. So when. How do you just stop. Two people/who

DORA: (   ).

ED: If you loved me one month/ago

DORA: Ed

ED: Do you love me? *(Pause.) Did* you?

DORA: (   ).

ED: (   )?

DORA: Yes (but) —

ED: So when did you stop.

DORA: (   ). *(Pause.)*

ED: I'm sorry.

DORA: I'm gonna/leave, Ed.

ED: OK, wait. Wait. I got this idea. It's a way you can help me. It's a really good idea. *(Dora looks at Ed. Ed looks at Dora.)* I wanna. OK. Ready?

DORA: (   ).

ED: I wanna rob the Blockbuster.

DORA: — What?

ED: How much is it before you put the final night's total in the safe?

DORA: Ed.

ED: Corporation, won't feel a thing. A couple thousand, right? At closing, so easy, just you in the store —

DORA: No, Ed!

ED: I know there's all those cameras and stuff, but I put on a mask or whatever, we make it look like an actual robbery, like, with a gun and stuff, simple!

DORA: A *gun?*

ED: I have one. I got one.

DORA: You have a *gun?*

ED: What if I get into trouble with John? (What if I have to do) Some ghetto shit? *(Pause.)*

DORA: I'm going, Ed.

ED: You're gonna go. You're just gonna go.

DORA: *(Rising.)* Yeah.

ED: All right. Whatever. *(Starts removing clothes.)* Thanks for the help!

DORA: What are you doing?

ED: (I'm gonna) Take a swim. You wanna?

DORA: Fuck you. *(Dora starts to exit. Ed stands naked, laughs.)*

ED: You know you want me. That's why you're leaving! *(She keeps going till she is offstage. Calling:)* You know that's why you're leaving! Come on, come swimming with me. *(Pause. Dora is offstage. He yells:)* WHY DON'T YOU COME BACK HERE AND COME SWIMMING WITH ME. WHY DON'T YOU COME BACK AND SUCK MY DICK LIKE YOU USED TO! *(Long pause. He's still watching. Screaming.)* WHY DON'T YOU COME BACK AND TELL ME YOU LOVE ME. *(Hold.)*

THE DAZZLE
Richard Greenberg

Seriocomic
Homer and Milly, thirties

> The Dazzle *is a wild, dark comedy about the notorious Collyer brothers. Homer, a lawyer, is the more functional of the two. Here, he is trying to persuade a woman named Milly to marry his brother.*

HOMER: Welcome, Miss Ashmore, welcome, welcome, once again, to our home.

MILLY: Where is your brother?

HOMER: No, don't worry, it's just us. May I pour you some tea?

MILLY: I want *nothing.*

HOMER: *(Pours her tea.)* All right. You don't have to get huffy about —

MILLY: Where could he have possibly gone without you?

HOMER: An afternoon recital for ladies . . . in the *drawing* room of a *lady* —

MILLY: How did you persuade him to do that?

HOMER: I explained to him our finances — the condition our finances — sugar?

MILLY: No.

HOMER: *(Drops four lumps into the cup.)* I explained to him that the money they were offering was awfully good — I *reasoned* with him, I made him *see* that —

MILLY: How did you get him to go?

HOMER: I hit him *(Beat.)*

MILLY: No. Really.

HOMER: Well, you have to.

MILLY: No. Really.

HOMER: Well, it's Langley —

MILLY: You didn't hit him —

HOMER: He responds beautifully to physical violence — he always has —
he becomes an angel of docility. *(Pause.)*

MILLY: That sort of thing doesn't happen here.

HOMER: Doesn't it?

MILLY: You know, Mr. — Homer, I have been trying in these last weeks
to figure you out — to sift and winnow through your behavior to
me — its violent, even perverse swings — and after careful consid-
eration, I have come to the conclusion that you are extremely hard
to read.

HOMER: I shouldn't be — I'm an open book — well, no, I'm more like
an open *stack*, really — *Madame Bovary, c'est moi* — and also everybody else in the damn library —

MILLY: You know, I'm not untrained in psychology — and —

HOMER: I *know* this about you — you are utterly *à la mode* — that's your
ferocious attraction —

MILLY: What do you think of me, really? What do you think the relationship
is among the three of us? How would you put it into words? How
would you characterize it?

HOMER: I would say . . . You're a silly little rich trollop who likes to tease
our cocks.

MILLY: Mr. Collyer!

HOMER: OK, let me try another one:
You are . . . the spirit of the avant-garde incarnate . . . a quester
after the new; it is by the efforts of you and your likes that the fallen,
fractured, machine-wrecked world will once again be made whole.

MILLY: . . . That's better.

HOMER: I don't know. I think before I was closer to the mark.

MILLY: I can leave —

HOMER: But you won't. Oh listen: You're our *enzyme*. In your presence,
reactions take place.

MILLY: Why did you ask me here today?

HOMER: I want to know your intentions toward my brother. *(Pause. She
laughs.)* No, no, no. Answer.

MILLY: How can I answer that? Intentions are had *toward* women not *by*
them.

HOMER: In this case, we'll have to make an exception.

MILLY: It's not possible —

HOMER: It simply has to be; you'll have to propose to him —

MILLY: First of all, the presumption of you to assume I'm in any way interest —

HOMER: Oh, don't fake —

MILLY: — and even if I were —

HOMER: Is there under all that — persiflage — a hard little throbbing nugget of convention that really runs you? *(Beat.)*

MILLY: Will I have to sink to my knee?

HOMER: Save that for after the wedding.

MILLY: You're mad —

HOMER: Well, how *else* is it going to happen? Do you expect to start him in your direction, in some way?

MILLY: Well, maybe I do. *(Beat.)*

HOMER: Huh. I suppose I could *hit* him.

MILLY: Flattering.

HOMER: Oh, it isn't you — it's anything — anything — you can't get him to — that he *washes* regularly is only due to me — I am his — prime mover! — that's —

MILLY: Then — does this mean — you *want* him to marry me?

HOMER: I want the two of you to become engaged.

MILLY: And to marry?

HOMER: Oh no — I'll scuttle that.

MILLY: You'll —

HOMER: Or *fail* to —

MILLY: Which?

HOMER: There's no telling — that's the marvelous part!

MILLY: Then — are we — allies, antagonists — what —

HOMER: Antagonists, I hope — *(Sincerely like an offer of friendship.)* I *want* us to be antagonists.

MILLY: Do you hate me, Homer?

HOMER: Not at all.

MILLY: Why do you act as though you do?

HOMER: Because it makes for a better scene! *(Beat.)*
   Oh — look — you excite me — you — *excite* me —

MILLY: I know —

HOMER: I am my brother's accountant — do you know? I am: that. *(Beat.)*
I was — when I was — a child — my mother — oh let me start with
her: My mother was a woman of taste.

MILLY: *(Satisfied smile.)* I knew your mother would come into this.

HOMER: If you only knew — the epic saga of my Aunt Prudy's cheap lac-
quered vase — the infamy of its entry into our house — the diatribes
my mother launched against it on a daily basis — and the way she
managed — accidentally and in full view of my aunt — to sweep it
off its pedestal and smash it into a thousand pieces!

MILLY: So?

HOMER: So? Well. I'm not sure . . . That story has always seemed to have
a point.

MILLY: "I am my brother's accountant."

HOMER: Yes! When I was quite young, my mother said to me, "Homer,
you are *for* your brother." Can you imagine? It was a kind of mani-
festo for my life; she was not a casual woman, there was an aura of
fatality about the way she'd pour the *coffee* — so when she said —
and I still so young — "You are *for* your brother" — I knew at once
that my life would be devoted to dodging this proposition — because
you see — I wanted my own life.

MILLY: Of course.

HOMER: And had it . . .
I *do* have — I mean, the *past* . . . is *real* . . . it doesn't seem so, but it
is. It is *true.*

MILLY: I know. I am the ruin of that truth. *(Beat.)*

HOMER: I'm sorry.

MILLY: That's all right. I'm better . . . since Vienna . . . *(Beat.)* Tell me:
How did you get from there to here? How did you end up tending
to him, after you'd made your escape?

HOMER: Oh. Well. Fraternal love is a powerful —

MILLY: No, really.

HOMER: He was spending all our money.

MILLY: I *knew* it was money!

HOMER: All our property is held jointly, and it was made known to me that he was squandering it — and I came and took over. *(Pause.)* In addition, fraternal love is a powerful —

MILLY: How *much* money is there?

HOMER: Less and less.

MILLY: Are you in danger of losing everything?

HOMER: Oh, I hope so!

MILLY: Homer.

HOMER: I don't care what happens as long as something does. My brother's life is . . . one of . . . piecemeal intensities; I watch him. Some nights — weeknights — I watch him, right around seven P.M. — that poignant, Booth Tarkington hour when people come home. Do you know, sometimes he cries? I can see him *weeping* for it — and I think as long as this still happens, then life is possible. But opportunity passes. I have forgotten how I got from there to here. *(Beat.)*

MILLY: Then I would be the mistress of this house.

HOMER: Yes, sure, fine.

MILLY: I would be in charge of the servants —

HOMER: We don't have servants; every two weeks an old blind woman comes to spit on the dust —

MILLY: There will *be* servants.

HOMER: We can't keep them.

MILLY: With me here, that won't be a problem. I'll be in charge.

HOMER: Yes, fine.

MILLY: Everything will have to change.

HOMER: "Change"! The most thrilling of all words!

MILLY: Now about my money.

HOMER: And there's the second most thrilling —

MILLY: It would have to remain my money. I mean, the marriage contract would have to be accompanied by another, rather more realistic document that my lawyers will arrange. So that in the event of anything at all happening, my property would never be imperiled.

HOMER: You do *love* my brother?

MILLY: Passionately, romantically. I'll call on my lawyer tonight.

HOMER: Fine — I love lawyers — I am one!
You won't . . . ?

MILLY: Finish.

HOMER: — love him too much, will you? Or understand him too completely and let him know it? That wouldn't play well.

MILLY: I understand him implicitly. He is an artist, therefore turbulent, strange, possessed by passions unknown to the common run of people. He needs to be cosseted, indulged, and surreptitiously held in check.

HOMER: Oh, good! Nothing to worry about.

MILLY: *(To herself.)* Marriage to him will be a great spite to my family. *(Beat.)* Well. What a lovely visit this has been!

HOMER: So much accomplished.

MILLY: Yes. *(Lang enters, ashen-faced and wobbly.)*

LANG: Homer — !

HOMER: Lang —

LANG: I can't — I can't —

HOMER: What is it?

LANG: Don't make me do that again — don't make me do that again — don't make me do that again — don't make me —

HOMER: What happened?

LANG: I can't tell you that — I can't tell you that — you *know* it's too much to tell — *(Homer is holding him now, propping him up.)* Please don't make me do it again.

HOMER: No, I won't — no — never — no I won't —

LANG: Hello, Milly.

MILLY: Hello, Lang.

LANG: Why is she here?

HOMER: Oh. We were making some plans?

LANG: Plans!? Do they include me?

HOMER: Only to a negligible degree. Listen, why don't you go up now? Have a bath. I'll bring you something on a tray.

LANG: Yes. Yes, all right. *(Homer helps him out of the room. Left unsupported, he walks, wobbly, off.)*

MILLY: Sweet to watch you walk him like that.

HOMER: Fraternal love is a powerful thing.

MILLY: I must to my lawyer, before it's too late.

HOMER: Yes. What time is it anyway?

MILLY: *(Consults her watch.)* Almost seven.

HOMER: Seven.

MILLY: Yes.

HOMER: Seven P.M.

MILLY: Yes.

HOMER: And I'm in it! I'm in it!

DREAMING OF NORTON
Casey McCabe

Dramatic
Toby, midthirties; Karen, twenties

> *A trashed motel room just off the highway in the middle of Kansas.*
> *Toby is an insurance claims adjuster in his mid-thirties, but he is*
> *wildly uncomfortable in the white-collar world. Karen is a young*
> *waitress at the nearby diner, packed into tight jeans and a Jose Cuervo*
> *T-shirt. As the scene opens they are dancing to Madonna's "Like a*
> *Virgin" playing on a portable stereo and drinking heavily. They have*
> *just met.*

TOBY: *(Singing.)* . . . *Like a virgin. Touched for the very first time. Like a vir-ir-irigin* . . . *(Now talking.)* Like a virgin. Now that's a good one. Like being kinda pregnant. Or sorta dead. Whatta you think, Karen . . .

KAREN: I told you, it's "car-EN."

TOBY: OK, car-EN . . . *(Thinks about it for a moment.)* Did your parents really name you that?

KAREN: No. I hated Karen. So I changed it to car-EN when I turned sixteen.

TOBY: How long ago was that?

KAREN: Long enough.

TOBY: Wanted to be kinda unique, eh?

KAREN: Beats Karen.

TOBY: So car-EN, do you ever, you know, feel like a virgin?

KAREN: *(Sarcastic.)* What do you think?

TOBY: No, think about it for a moment. Maybe it's like the wise poet here suggests. Virginity is a state of mind.

KAREN: You're interested in my mind . . . that's very sweet.

TOBY: I never said that. *(He dances behind her and begins working his hands up over her stomach and onto her breasts. Singing:)* . . . *touched for the very first tiiiime* . . .

(Karen stops dancing, patiently indulges his clumsy groping.)

KAREN: You certainly know how to make a girl feel like an innocent flower.

TOBY: That's why they call me Dr. Love.

KAREN: I thought it was Mr. Johnson.

TOBY: Did I say Johnson? I meant Smith.

KAREN: Right.

> *(She casually removes his hands from her body and walks over to the table, now covered with various bottles, cups, ice cubes, stereo player, and stray cassettes. She takes an ice cube and rubs it around her collarbone. Toby continues dancing by himself.)*

KAREN: I am so hot.

TOBY: Now you're flattering yourself.

KAREN: You know what I meant.

TOBY: I'll decide if you're hot or not.

> *(She pops the ice cube into her mouth and grins at him.)*

TOBY: OK. You're hot.

> *(Karen turns down the music and begins mixing herself a drink. Toby continues his rather spastic solo dance.)*

KAREN: Can I get you anything, light of my life?

TOBY: I'm fine for the moment, honey. But moments being fleeting as they are, go ahead and fix me one of those cute little seven and sevens of yours.

KAREN: *(Fixing his drink.)* You're not from around here at all, are you?

TOBY: California, originally.

KAREN: I figured.

TOBY: Los Angeles to start. Then to Seattle, to Denver, to Wichita to wherever the hell we are now, of course.

KAREN: Highway 36, just out of Smith Center, Kansas. Did you know you're only twelve miles from the geographical center of the United States?

TOBY: Well as a matter of fact, yes. You see I'm slowly working my way down the lower intestine of this great country of ours. In a few years I expect to be just another turd floating in the Gulf of Mexico.

KAREN: And let me guess . . . you're not a land speculator for Phillips Petroleum after all.

TOBY: *(Grinning.)* Sounded good, didn't it?

(He stops dancing, comes over to get his drink.)

KAREN: No. I wasn't impressed if that's what you mean.

(She hands him his drink, they perform an awkward little toast. A tone of sincerity enters her banter.)

KAREN: But I thought you were funny. And you don't take yourself too seriously. That's kind of refreshing, you know . . . what with me having to work the night shift over at that sad little Happy Chef.

TOBY: *(With mock suspicion.)* If that is indeed where you work.

KAREN: I waited on your table.

TOBY: Yes, of course.

KAREN: As if someone would lie about that. Speaking of lying, Mr. Johnson . . .

TOBY: That's Smith . . . no, make that "Smythe." Eh, car-EN?

KAREN: Toby. I know that's your real first name.

TOBY: Really. How?

KAREN: By the look on your face when you said it.

TOBY: I had no idea.

KAREN: I also know you're not married.

(He waves his ringless finger before her.)

KAREN: Oh, it's not that you don't have a ring, I mean any genius can figure out how to take off a stupid ring. It's just . . . oh I don't know, something about you.

TOBY: Something no woman would marry. You are beautiful and wise, young car-EN. I sure hope I tipped you big.

KAREN: Grossly. And I appreciated it.

(Toby kisses her neck. Karen pulls away, by no means rejecting, merely prolonging.)

TOBY: Shy?

KAREN: I followed a total stranger to his motel room.

(He mulls over this bit of logic and smiles.)

KAREN: So what'd you do to your arm, anyway?

TOBY: Old napalm scar . . . Tet Offensive . . . 'Nam. You're too young to know about any of that.

KAREN: So are you. Looks to me like another case of traveling salesman elbow.

TOBY: God I hate this place.

KAREN: Tell me then, what do you really do? Just straight out. God knows it doesn't matter to me.

TOBY: This week? This week I'm an insurance claims adjuster. *(He studies her reaction. There is none.)* As if someone would lie about that. *(Painfully frank.)* No honey, I work out of an office in Wichita. The headquarters of American Providence, purveyors of life, home, auto, and casualty insurance. This is one of my regions. You know that big storm that tore through here last week?

KAREN: Hard to miss.

TOBY: Every tree limb that broke off, every Goddamn hailstone that fell, went through somebody's new Buick or stained glass window or killed a dog or a show pony or something. We're really up to our ass in paperwork. It's crazy, crazy . . . *(Trails off and takes a drink.)* Livin' in a place like this. Jesus.

(Karen sits on the edge of the bed. Toby's lust has cooled.)

KAREN: You don't look like an insurance man.

TOBY: Thanks.

KAREN: My dad lost a Morton building and the windshield on his truck.

TOBY: Uh-huh.

KAREN: He was insured with State Farm.

TOBY: Really.

KAREN: Got his check already.

TOBY: Great.

(Karen leans back on the bed, propped up on her elbows, twirling her shoe on her foot. The game of pursuit has shifted.)

KAREN: No, Toby. You don't look like an insurance man. Oh, I believe you well enough. You just don't look like an insurance man, that's all. You're what I'd call a rounder. A guy who lies about things that don't really matter. Acts kinda dangerous, even though he ain't. Always sucking hind tit and laughing about it. A regular rounder. That's why I followed you here. Against all good and holy logic. *(She stares at him for a long moment.)* Do you plan on making love to me?

(He looks up at her slowly, his face contorted in distaste. She is stealing his thunder.)

KAREN: I kinda need to know.

EVOLUTION
Jonathan Marc Sherman

Comic
Henry and Hope, midtwenties

> *Henry has taken a hiatus from writing his thesis on Charles Dar-*
> *win. He is in Los Angeles, where his uncanny pop-culture illiteracy*
> *leads to his meteoric rise in the entertainment industry. Hope is his*
> *girlfriend, who has come with him to la-la land but who has seri-*
> *ous doubts about Henry's recent career choices.*

> *Henry's office. Henry is sitting with his feet on his desk. Hope is star-*
> *ing at a letter in a frame that sits on top of an exquisite dark cherry*
> *wood, antique bookshelf, no more than three feet high. The telephone*
> *is the only other thing on top of the bookshelf. Quality booze in crys-*
> *tal decanters and a set of glasses sit patiently on the bottom shelf.*
> *On the middle shelf are a few scripts for "Adam and Eve" and "Belly*
> *Buttons" episodes, along with a dictionary, a thesaurus, and a Bible.*
> *Hope's five portraits of Henry's face from her dorm room are hung*
> *in a straight line across the back wall, each lit from above by a sep-*
> *arate lamp, each staring down at the scene. An antique mirror sits*
> *on Henry's desk. His office is finally finished, and so is he — ex-*
> *pensive suit, hair slicked back just so, clear-lensed designer eyeglasses*
> *for effect.*

HENRY: *Guess.*

HOPE: I have *no idea* . . .

HENRY: Nine thousand dollars.

HOPE: *(Beat.)* Oh.

HENRY: Actually, eight thousand nine hundred and fifty dollars, to be exact.
(Beat.) Plus tax, of course.

HOPE: Of course.

HENRY: Can you believe that? I mean, he wrote it in 1870, Charles Darwin sat down at his desk or whatever and wrote that letter in *1870,*

and all I had to do was give a few thousand dollars to these auto-graph dealers in the *Beverly Center,* of all places — they authenticated it, framed it, put a photo of him in there — then I paid them some money, and now I *own* that. It's *mine.* That piece of history is *mine.*

HOPE: That's great.

HENRY: Yeah. It is. It's *great. (Beat.)* I bought it before the show got picked up and spun off and all . . . I bought it *recklessly,* without *restraint . . .* I mean, buying a Darwin letter in the Goddamn *Beverly* Center . . . I can't even tell you . . . it was such an extraordinary feeling of *free-dom . . .*

HOPE: This isn't time off to get focused anymore, is it?

HENRY: No.

HOPE: No. That's what I thought. *(Beat.)* I was thinking, on the plane, thinking about when we met. *(Beat.)* Thinking about the book.

HENRY: The book . . .

HOPE: *Your* book.

HENRY: Hmm . . .

HOPE: Do you still think about it?

HENRY: Yeah. *(Beat.)* Yeah, I think about it.

HOPE: I didn't know if you still did.

HENRY: I think about pouring my heart into something ten people would read, something that's completely irrelevant five years after it's writ-ten, something that's only distinction might very possibly be that it lacks a common *vowel.* I think about all the remaindered books, all the dusty old books on dead people's bookshelves, or sold for fifty cents on the sidewalk by some *guy.* Or thrown in the trash. You've got to be truly great and truly lucky to even dream of lasting. But even that . . . Darwin's *Origin of the Species* has been around for a hundred and forty years, and on the map of time, a hundred and forty years is: *BLIP.* That's all. Barely anything. Eventually, Darwin won't exist anymore. There won't even be a trace. BLIP. BLIP.

HOPE: That's cute, Henry. BLIP. That is *cute.* All this time I've known you and never once did I detect you had this amazing capacity for ratio-nalizing bullshit. Look at what you're *doing.*

HENRY: And what are *you* doing? What are *you* doing, Hope? Spending daddy's money, slapping colors on a canvas, being as self-indulgent as the next college student, with insulated ideals. Why do you paint, Hope? Tell me, why? What *for?* Why is it better than what I'm doing? It all comes down to the same basics, and they're not much: living and breathing and eating and sleeping and fucking and working and feeling and *dying.* And *Thank God* I woke up, *Thank God* I looked around at the world surrounding me, *Thank God* I took some action.

HOPE: Since when do you believe in God?

HENRY: Since God put money in my pocket and gave me a *purpose.*

HOPE: What do you *want?*

HENRY: I *want* to continue being successful.

HOPE: But what do you *want?*

HENRY: I want an Emmy Award.

HOPE: But what do you *want?*

HENRY: I want you to stop talking. Splitting headache. You're driving me *nuts.* And I don't *have* to answer to you. To *anybody.*

HOPE: Listen to yourself, Henry.

HENRY: *Gladly.* What's that I'm hearing? That I'm ambitious. Boo-hoo. Name me one solid thing that isn't. History of life, darling. Not a building would get built, not a child born, not a *Goddamn thing done* if somebody didn't decide to swim against the tide, break a rule, fuck the order, reach for something they weren't given and maybe shouldn't ever get. Find me somebody without ambition and I'll find you somebody *dead.* Imagine an unambitious God. Not so easy. Not so easy at all. Ambition, evolution, same fucking thing.

HOPE: *(Beat.)* You should be in *intensive* psychotherapy.

HENRY: As Robert Redford said, "Other people have analysis. I have Utah."

HOPE: What does Utah have to do with *you?*

HENRY: His Utah is my new car.

HOPE: You used to quote *Darwin.*

HENRY: Robert Redford's better *looking. (Beat.)* I have no intention of ending up like my father, Hope. No intention whatsoever.

HOPE: Your father is an expert in his field, Henry, he just . . .

HENRY: *(Manic.)* And *what* a field. He's an expert in his field? Yes, true, but that's not *all* he is. Oh, no. He's crazy, he's locked up, he's numb — he's an expert in his field — he's an insane fucking *semantics* professor who never let me watch Saturday morning cartoons, or listen to the radio,

or go to fucking *grade* school for Chrissakes. Expert in his field —
that and a nickel and a fucking cup of *coffee* —

HOPE: *(Lightly crying.)* You're *scaring* me, Henry.

HENRY: *(Beat.)* I'm sorry . . . I just . . . I'm sorry.

HOPE: Me, too. *(Beat.)* You know, last week, my therapist informed me
that you are officially the most powerful person in my life. You em-
body the defining qualities of all three members of my nuclear family. You were always my Daddy substitute — protective male, smart.
And you always cuddled with me, like my mother did when I was a
little girl and couldn't sleep. So all that you needed to do was get some
Ernie stuff into the mix. And you've certainly succeeded. I think it's
safe to say you've overachieved in that area. You have the ability to
enrage me just like he did all throughout my childhood. Dad and
Mom and lousy kid brother, all-in-one. Add water and stir. Presto.
Instant Henry. Highly toxic.

THE FERRY
Ryan Hill

Comic
Man and Woman, could be any age

Two riders on the Staten Island Ferry meet for the first time.

MAN: You from Staten Island?
WOMAN: I already told you —
MAN: 'Cause I'm from Staten Island.
WOMAN: No, I'm not from Staten Island.
MAN: You work in Staten Island?
WOMAN: No.
MAN: Where you from?
WOMAN: I'm from Iowa.
MAN: —
WOMAN: —
MAN: —
WOMAN: —
MAN: Isn't that in Suffolk County?
WOMAN: No.
MAN: Oh. I ain't never been there. Where do you live, if you don't live in
    Staten Island?
WOMAN: I live in Manhattan.
MAN: Oh.
WOMAN: You ever been there?
MAN: No.
WOMAN: —
MAN: —
WOMAN: —
MAN: Is that in Suffolk County?
WOMAN: You're serious?
MAN: —

WOMAN: You don't know where Manhattan is?

MAN: I ain't no worldly guy. I'm just a simple guy from —

BOTH: Staten Island.

WOMAN: I know. Where did you get on this ferry?

MAN: Staten Island.

WOMAN: No, just a couple of minutes ago, you got on the ferry, right?

MAN: No.

WOMAN: What do you mean, "no"? You're standing here, aren't you?

MAN: Yeah.

WOMAN: Then you got on the ferry in Manhattan.

MAN: No. I got on the ferry in Staten Island.

WOMAN: Wait a minute, you just rode the ferry from Staten Island to Manhattan and now you're riding it back?

MAN: Back from where?

WOMAN: Look behind you.

MAN: Why?

WOMAN: That's Manhattan.

MAN: Where?

WOMAN: See all those buildings? See that island?

MAN: Yeah.

WOMAN: That's Manhattan.

MAN: Oh.

WOMAN: So this ferry runs between Manhattan and Staten Island.

MAN: No.

WOMAN: "No" what?

MAN: This ferry runs between Staten Island and Staten Island.

WOMAN: But it stops between trips. It crosses the water and goes to Manhattan, then goes back to Staten Island.

MAN: Oh, yeah. It does, but it's not important.

WOMAN: Didn't you wonder why the boat stopped and everyone got off?

MAN: No.

WOMAN: Didn't you think that was strange to do if it hadn't stopped somewhere important?

MAN: No.

WOMAN: Why?

MAN: 'Cause it does that all day.

WOMAN: Do you ride this thing all day?

MAN: No.

WOMAN: —

MAN: I go home at night.

WOMAN: So you ride the Staten Island ferry all day.

MAN: No. I get up in the morning, then get on the ferry.

WOMAN: And you've never gotten off in Manhattan?

MAN: Listen, lady. I'm sorry, but you're not making much sense. The ferry goes in one direction. It goes from Staten Island to Staten Island. Anything in between doesn't matter.

WOMAN: What do you think's going on behind you? In all those buildings? What do you think's happening back there?

MAN: Doesn't matter.

WOMAN: That's the heart and soul of this country, the machinery that makes the world go around is back there. Can't you feel the energy?

MAN: Doesn't matter.

WOMAN: How can you say that?

MAN: Because it doesn't matter.

WOMAN: Those towers, all those people . . . All the sweat and tears it took to build this country is condensed right there. That is the island of infinite possibilities. People from every corner of this planet come to this skyline because they know hard work and talent will pay off. They know anything is possible. How can you say it doesn't matter? That's progress, the city of dreams.

MAN: You want to talk about forward, but you keep looking backwards.

WOMAN: Fine. What's forward for you?

MAN: That's forward.

WOMAN: And what's that?

MAN: Staten Island.

WOMAN: —

MAN: —

WOMAN: You know what that is?

MAN: Statue of Liberty.

WOMAN: And you don't know what Manhattan is?

MAN: —

WOMAN: Wait a minute, how do you know where Suffolk County is?

MAN: That's where my mom grew up.

WOMAN: You've never been there?

MAN: No.

WOMAN: Don't you have any relatives or anything back there? Grandparents you visited?

MAN: Nope.

WOMAN: Why not?

MAN: They all live in Staten Island now.

WOMAN: —

MAN: You hungry?

WOMAN: No.

MAN: 'Cause I'm gonna have dinner.

WOMAN: You bring food with you?

MAN: Don't you?

WOMAN: What do you have in there?

MAN: Some grapes. Chicken. Ham sandwich.

WOMAN: Where did you get that stuff?

MAN: Staten —

WOMAN: I mean what store?

MAN: The grocery store.

WOMAN: Do you have a job?

MAN: What do you mean?

WOMAN: Where did you get the money to buy that food?

MAN: What do you mean?

WOMAN: You bought that food, right?

MAN: —

WOMAN: Did you steal that?

MAN: What do you mean?

WOMAN: Jesus, you stole all that? You're a thief.

MAN: Listen, lady. I don't know where you're from, but things are different out here on Staten Island.

WOMAN: Not that different.

MAN: How would you know? Are you from Staten Island?

WOMAN: No.

MAN: Then don't criticize our ways of doing things.

WOMAN: Stealing isn't legal no matter where it is.

MAN: Call it what you want. I've got food.

WOMAN: So do I, but I didn't steal it.

MAN: You've got food?

WOMAN: Yes.

MAN: Show me.

WOMAN: *(She pulls out a candy bar.)* And I didn't steal it.

MAN: Good for you.

WOMAN: —

MAN: —

WOMAN: What's that over there?

MAN: I don't know.

WOMAN: It's Brooklyn.

MAN: Whatever.

WOMAN: You've never heard of Brooklyn?

MAN: Maybe.

WOMAN: What about that, you know what that is?

MAN: A park.

WOMAN: Do you know what the city's called?

MAN: No.

WOMAN: That's Jersey City. And all of that is New Jersey.

MAN: Sure.

WOMAN: And back over there is Newark. And further up the river is the Bronx, and further up the other river is Queens. And past New Jersey is Pennsylvania, that way is Philadelphia, Pittsburgh's that way. Massachusetts and Boston are up that way, by Connecticut, Rhode Island, Vermont, New Hampshire, Maine, upstate New York — you have heard of New York, right?
(Man shrugs while eating.)

WOMAN: This is ludicrous. You've never heard of Washington, D.C.? Our capital? Baltimore? Maryland? Virginia? You ever heard of Florida? Do you know Disneyland?

MAN: Something about a big mouse, right?

WOMAN: What about . . . Chicago? Minnesota? Denver? New Mexico? Mexico? California? Have you ever heard of Los Angeles? Do you know what Hollywood is?

MAN: It's a big wooden sign.

WOMAN: Well . . . yes . . . but that's a part of a city called Los Angeles.

MAN: So?

WOMAN: So? So, it's important to know these things.

MAN: Why?

WOMAN: It gives us a sense of where we are.

MAN: I know where I am.

WOMAN: Yeah, you're on the ferry. But don't you want to know where other people come from?

MAN: I know where you're from, you told me. You're from someplace near Suffolk County.

WOMAN: Iowa is not near Suffolk County.

MAN: Oh. Then where is it?

WOMAN: See? See what I mean? If you knew what these places were, you'd be able to identify people.

MAN: Identify them how?

WOMAN: Well, you'd be able to know that I'm from Iowa. And you'd know what that means.

MAN: What does that mean?

WOMAN: I mean to say that, you'd be able to know me better.

MAN: How's that?

WOMAN: Well, you'd know what people are like there.

MAN: What's it like in Iowa?

WOMAN: Well, Iowa's in the Midwest. There's lots of rural areas. Lots of farms. It's not real progressive. There's a lot of corn. People don't think Iowans are very smart. Um . . . I don't know.

MAN: So if I knew what Iowa was, and you told me you were from Iowa, then I'd know right away that you're a farmer, you're not very progressive, you're not very smart, and you eat corn.

WOMAN: That's not what I meant.

MAN: Do you like corn?

WOMAN: That's not the point.

MAN: Are you progressive?

WOMAN: I'd like to think so.

MAN: Are you a farmer?

WOMAN: No.

MAN: Then, since you're none of those things, and I know you're smart, what good does it do me to know where Iowa is?

WOMAN: OK. OK, so that's not a good example. But what if you meet someone from another country. It would help to know where they're from.

MAN: What other country?

WOMAN: Say a man from Japan came up to you. If you knew he was from Japan, you'd know that —

MAN: He liked corn?

WOMAN: No.

MAN: He doesn't like corn?

WOMAN: No, that's not the point.

MAN: What does he eat?

WOMAN: I don't know . . . sushi and rice and dumplings and things.

MAN: So I'd know that. What else would I know.

WOMAN: You'd know you have to treat him different.

MAN: Why?

WOMAN: Well, because he's from Japan.

MAN: Why would I treat him differently?

WOMAN: Because . . . well . . . he's not from here.

MAN: You're not from Staten Island and I treat you like you're from Staten Island.

WOMAN: Alright. That's not my point.

MAN: I'm sorry, lady, but I've missed your point.

WOMAN: My point is that if you know where someone is from, you automatically know some things about them that can help you act differently toward them.

MAN: —

WOMAN: —

MAN: OK.

WOMAN: See?

MAN: Why would I want to treat people differently?

WOMAN: —

MAN: —

WOMAN: Because people are different.

MAN: But they're still people.

WOMAN: Sure, but . . . not everyone's from Staten Island.

MAN: I know that.

WOMAN: —

MAN: So, how should I treat you?

WOMAN: Like normal.

MAN: What's normal?

WOMAN: —

MAN: —

WOMAN: Like I'm from Staten Island.

(The man smiles.)

MAN: Want a grape?

(Blackout.)

FISHER KING
Don Nigro

Dramatic
Bel, seventeen; Perce, slightly older

> *In the last autumn of the American Civil War, Bel Rhys, who lives*
> *with her father Merlin in a tattered revival tent in the woods, is*
> *very upset that her brother Rudd, a Union soldier, has, after a brief*
> *visit, had to return to the war. Perce Welsh, a country boy who's been*
> *following Major Pendragon and his men, the group Rudd's with, in*
> *hopes of joining up, comes upon Bel, who is pounding on her pump*
> *organ in frustration, watches her, unseen by her. She bangs on the*
> *organ a few more times, then stops.*

PERCE: That's a real nice song there.
BEL: *(Startled.)* What?
PERCE: What's the name of that?
BEL: I don't know.
PERCE: Is this some kind of church?
BEL: Sort of.
PERCE: There's a organ.
BEL: So?
PERCE: I never seen an organ.
BEL: Then how do you know what it is?
PERCE: I'm smarter than I look.
BEL: Uh huh. Are you with Major Pendragon?
PERCE: Yeah.
BEL: They went off that way.
PERCE: I thought I smelled bread. You bakin' bread?
BEL: You ain't no soldier.
PERCE: Maybe I come for a prayer meetin'.
BEL: We don't have no prayer meetings no more.
PERCE: Your tent's a mite raggedy. Preacher run off?
BEL: He ate something in the woods and got touched in the head by the
    Holy Spirit, or whoever. He saw an angel, talks to him and stuff.

PERCE: He saw an angel?

BEL: That's what he says. He don't care much for real folks now. Just draws dirty pictures and eats weeds.

PERCE: My ma saw an angel once. Said he touched her right titty. Course, she had drank four bottles of cough medicine at the time, so I don't know. You play that thing good?

BEL: I don't know. Loud.

PERCE: Will you play me somethin'?

BEL: I don't feel like it.

PERCE: You're a real soft-lookin' girl. Real pretty skin. I like that. You all by yourself here?

BEL: *(Getting more and more uneasy.)* No, I'm not by myself. My pa is just over in the bushes, eatin' weeds. And my brother is a soldier. He just went off that way, but he's comin' right back, he said. Whole mess of soldiers, and Major Pendragon. With guns. They went to chop wood. Daddy got a big ax, a great big one, and my brother and the soldiers is out there with him. Ten or twelve of them. Sixteen, maybe twenty.

PERCE: I don't hear no choppin'.

BEL: They're doin' it quiet, so as not to scare off the squirrels. Maybe they're resting. Hey, Rudd?

PERCE: I don't think I ever in my life seen a prettier girl than you. All white, like an angel. All soft like a little animal. I look at you, it makes me feel like, I don't know, like —

BEL: You want some lemonade?

PERCE: Can I touch that?

BEL: No. What?

PERCE: Can I touch your organ?

BEL: No. You just keep over there. We used to have real nice services, except for the screamin' and yellin', people teachin' the little children to shriek out their sins for Jesus. People on their knees just bawlin' and blubberin' all over each other, full of sin and achin' to get healed. Pa used to heal folks, but he don't do that no more, just eats leaves. Don't you come near me. All that blubberin' and spittin'. I tried not to look. I just played the music. The music was all clean and good, it was just the people that made me feel dirty. I used to wish sometimes that Jesus would come and wash away all my sins, just give me a bath all over. Because sometimes I have real sinful thoughts. You stay right there.

PERCE: I just want to put my fingers on it.

BEL: *(Backing away from him, toward the organ.)* My brother is big and strong like Jesus and he could rip your nose right off your face, easy.

PERCE: I ain't gonna hurt you none. I'm your friend. God, you smell good.

BEL: Rudd? You come back here. RUDD.

PERCE: Don't be afraid. I wouldn't hurt you. You smell like my ma's box. She's got a old chocolate box she keeps all this junk in, dime-store rings and beads off old dresses and pieces of hair and it smells kinda like her and kinda like vanilla, you know? Can I just —

BEL: You're leadin' me to have sinful thoughts, now. You smell the sin, it smells like old jewelry boxes and the back room of the church where my daddy took me once and the preacher was puttin' on his robe and he looked like a skeleton in a black shroud, and the preacher leaned down to kiss me, and he said what a pretty girl I was, and all I could think of was sinful thoughts. You stay away from me or I'll call Jesus to protect me. I swear. You keep away from me. You just keep away. *(Perce has reached out one hand and holds it upright, palm toward her, close to one breast, not touching. Bel stares at him.)*

PERCE: I need to touch things. I don't see too good, sometimes. I get kind of lost in my head and I don't hear things like other people hear. I hear different things. Voices in my head. I got to touch things to make sure they're real. If I could just —

BEL: *(Not moving.)* Evil. I can smell evil. We got to fight it. Jesus never had no sinful thoughts. He never touched nobody at all.

PERCE: He did. To make them well. He touched them and they was healed. *(Perce touches her breast. She looks at him.)*

BEL: You feel like Jesus. Are you Jesus? It's all right if you're Jesus. It's not a sin if Jesus touches you on the breast. *(Bel kisses him. Then she looks at him.)*

PERCE: God. So soft. Like God. *(Perce kisses her, and Bel sits back on the keyboard of the organ. Strange organ noises. Lights fade as they get more involved and the organ noises get more bizarre and frantic.)*

JUVENILIA
Wendy MacLeod

Seriocomic
Brodie and Meredith, college students, about twenty to twenty-two

> *Brodie and Meredith are students at a high-level liberal arts college
> and are boyfriend/girlfriend. He's a "party animal"; she is, too. They
> have "issues" regarding their relationship. Brodie sits in the hallway
> outside the door, leaning against the wall, holding a fifth of bour-
> bon, waiting for Meredith. She appears, carrying a plastic grocery
> sack. Seeing him, she stops.*

MEREDITH: Did you chicken out?

BRODIE: No.

MEREDITH: Did you have an attack of conscience?

BRODIE: No.

MEREDITH: Lord knows you didn't feel bad when you slept with the *lunch
lady*.

BRODIE: You got even. You slept with the maintenance guy.
*(Meredith sits down next to him. Meredith pulls two beers out of the bag
and hands one to Brodie.)*

BRODIE: *(Raising his bottle.)* I'm cool.

MEREDITH: Where'd you get that?

BRODIE: Across the hall. The door was open.

MEREDITH: *(Wrestling with her cap.)* Fuck.

BRODIE: Here.
(Brodie takes the bottle and opens it with the opener on his penknife.)

MEREDITH: He was a *gardener*.

BRODIE: Lady Chatterley Goes to College.

MEREDITH: He had dirt under his fingernails. I thought I was going to get
e-coli.

BRODIE: Well you run that risk with the lunch lady too.

MEREDITH: Maybe *that's* why she gives you extra portions.

BRODIE: Yeah! She has been pushing the ground beef!

MEREDITH: Why are you here?

BRODIE: I got kicked out.

MEREDITH: Who kicked you out?

BRODIE: Angie.

MEREDITH: Why don't you go back in there and kiss her? It'll be like a Harlequin romance love-hate thing.

BRODIE: Because I'm not in the mood.

MEREDITH: You were in the mood for *Tiffany* . . .

BRODIE: Tiffany isn't a Christian!

MEREDITH: I thought you said Christians were *hot* . . .

BRODIE: Why don't *you* go have a threesome?

MEREDITH: With who?

BRODIE: *Anyone.*

MEREDITH: With you and Henry?

BRODIE: *No.*

MEREDITH: Why not?

BRODIE: Because he's my best friend.

MEREDITH: But if it were another guy you'd be fine with it.

BRODIE: If that's what you felt you had to do. I mean it's not like we're getting *married* . . .

MEREDITH: I hurt your feelings!

BRODIE: No you *didn't* . . .

MEREDITH: Just because I wasn't dreaming of the day you put the ring on my finger . . .

BRODIE: Meredith, I'm twenty years old! I'm not even fucking *thinking* about getting married!

(Meredith begins to mock sniffle.)

BRODIE: *Stop* it.

MEREDITH: It's because I mocked your hometown . . .

BRODIE: There happens to be plenty of money in Cincinnati . . .

MEREDITH: And your *Dad's* alma mater . . .

BRODIE: I don't know what the fuck you've been doing with me all this time if my circumstances are so laughable . . .

MEREDITH: I wanted your body!

BRODIE: Maybe that's all it is!

MEREDITH: You know, Henry is just capitalizing on the lust that you aroused . . .

BRODIE: Uh-huh.

MEREDITH: You're the one she wanted to sleep with. It was *obvious.*

BRODIE: This is a little *sick,* Meredith.

MEREDITH: What?

BRODIE: You! *Pimping* your boyfriend!

MEREDITH: I wouldn't ask you to do something you didn't *want* to do . . .

BRODIE: Yes you would! What *don't* you ask me to do!

MEREDITH: What do I ask you to do?

BRODIE: Back rubs, pickups, drop-offs, Fannie May chocolates, Midol, beer runs . . .

MEREDITH: Hey fuck you! *I* just did the beer run!

BRODIE: Only because you had an *agenda.*

MEREDITH: An agenda that *failed . . .*

BRODIE: Henry succeeded.

MEREDITH: Anybody can have a random hook up on Friday night! The challenge was a *three-way* with a *Christian!*

BRODIE: Hey, we should pitch that to Devon's dad. It could be the new *Survivor.*

MEREDITH: Soon you're going to get old, Brodie, so you might as well have a three-way while everyone still wants to sleep with you!

BRODIE: Fine, then let me have it with some sorority skank, who's giving it away *anyway . . .*

MEREDITH: Which sorority skank?

BRODIE: I don't know!

MEREDITH: What made you think of a sorority girl?

BRODIE: I go to college. There are *sororities* here . . .

MEREDITH: Which one would you do? If you *had* to choose . . .

BRODIE: I'm not answering that! It's a trick! I'll name a girl and you'll go fucking *postal.*

MEREDITH: That postal thing is so *tired . . .*

BRODIE: I'm sorry that my language disappoints you, but frankly, Meredith, what *doesn't* disappoint you?

MEREDITH: Answer the question, which sorority girl do you consider the most fuckable?

BRODIE: Emily Davies!

MEREDITH: Very funny . . .

BRODIE: "Eyebrow girl" . . .

MEREDITH: I know who it is so you might as well just say it!

BRODIE: You don't know who it fucking is!

MEREDITH: Tell me who it is or I'll stab you with your own knife I swear to God!

(Meredith grabs the penknife. They struggle. Meredith cuts Brodie.)

BRODIE: Jesus! Kate Cottrell, OK!

MEREDITH: The one with the big tits?

BRODIE: That's the one! They're huge! They make me want to fuck them!

MEREDITH: You've definitely been watching too much porn, Brodie . . .

BRODIE: That wasn't *porn,* that was *life!*

MEREDITH: You fucked Kate Cottrell's tits?

BRODIE: What if I did? It's not like you and I are getting *married* . . .

MEREDITH: Kate Cottrell is a joke! She carries a *purse!*

BRODIE: If you still loved me you wouldn't be telling me to sleep with Angela! You wouldn't be pimping your boyfriend!

MEREDITH: I'd rather do it than have *you* do it. At least then I have some *control.*

PENDRAGON

Don Nigro

Dramatic
Rhys, forty; Alison, twenties

> *John Rhys Pendragon, a respected but hard-drinking journalist, has come to Boise, Idaho, in 1910 to cover a prize fight and very reluctantly ended up getting deeply involved in a love triangle involving Isabel, a Basque girl once thought drowned, her fiancé Joe — who in his grief at her supposed death has taken comfort in the arms of the local tavern keeper's daughter, Alison McPherson, a sharp-tongued but good-hearted girl who is now pregnant by Joe, and can't decide what to do about it. Pendragon has spent a lot of time in her father's bar, trading insults with Alison, but there is more affection between them than either has been willing, up until this point, to admit.*

ALISON: I was hoping you'd be gone by now.

RHYS: So was I.

ALISON: Well, get lost then. I'm sick of looking at you.

RHYS: So am I. What are you going to do?

ALISON: About what?

RHYS: You're really not going to tell him?

ALISON: I don't want to talk about it.

RHYS: Alison, the kid's going to show up sooner or later, and then everybody's going to know, so what are you going to do about it?

ALISON: I'm going away.

RHYS: Where?

ALISON: I don't know where. Some place far.

RHYS: Great. Run away from all your friends and family, alone, pregnant, broke, out of work, in a strange place. Sounds like an excellent plan to me. Great future for the kid, too.

ALISON: I don't have any friends here except Bunny, and she can't help me.

The only family I've got is my father, and when he finds out, he'll disown me anyway. What do you care?

RHYS: I think you owe it to the boy to tell him.

ALISON: I don't owe him anything. I owe it to him not to.

RHYS: That makes no sense whatsoever.

ALISON: Why should I care what makes sense or doesn't make sense to some worthless newspaper drunk?

(Alison is crying. Rhys looks at her, then comes over to touch her shoulder. She pulls away angrily.)

ALISON: Get your filthy hands off me. Do you think because I let a foolish unhappy boy make love to me that I'm free for the taking?

RHYS: I'd think you'd be happy to have somebody around here that cares what happens to you.

ALISON: You don't care about anything. Give you a drink and you're in heaven. Writing garbage about punch-drunk has-been boxers, making smart-alecky remarks, chasing around little foreign girls half your age, no sense of responsibility, no morals, and very little brain. What an idiot.

(Pause.)

RHYS: Would you like to marry me?

ALISON: Pardon?

RHYS: I said, would you like to marry me?

ALISON: Marry you? Would I like to marry you?

RHYS: Yes. Would you like to marry me?

(Alison stares at him, dumfounded, for a moment, and then punches him very hard in the face, knocking him over a chair and onto the floor.)

Is that a yes or a no?

ALISON: Get out of here. Get out, or I'll get the shotgun from behind the bar and shoot you in the ass.

RHYS: I mean it.

ALISON: So do I.

RHYS: I'm serious.

ALISON: You're drunk.

RHYS: I am not drunk. One thing I have not gotten in Boise, Idaho, is drunk, and believe me, it hasn't been for lack of trying. But that notwithstanding —

ALISON: *(Pulling out the shotgun from behind the bar and levelling it at him.)* All right, now GET.

RHYS: *(Taking the gun away from her and slamming it on the bar.)* Will you put that stupid thing away and listen to me? I'll marry you. Do you understand what I'm saying? I will marry you.

ALISON: Who the hell asked you?

RHYS: What do you want? Do you want me to get down on my knees and beg? All right. *(He gets down on his knees and begins following her around the bar.)* Alison McPherson, I will marry you, and be your husband, and cleave unto you, and claim your child as my own, and raise it, and be as good to it and you as I am capable of, given my various mental and physical infirmities. Now, will you or won't you?

ALISON: Get up.

RHYS: I don't think I CAN get up.

ALISON: Do you really mean that?

RHYS: Yes, I think my knees died.

ALISON: I'm not talking about that, you blockhead. I mean, do you really want to marry me?

RHYS: What do you think, I like doing this? *(Trying to get up.)* Christ. I'll never broad jump again. *(He staggers. She helps him stay up.)* Yes, God help me, I do. I want to marry you.

ALISON: Why?

RHYS: Temporary insanity. The Lord spoke to me from out of the comet. How the hell do I know? What difference does it make?

ALISON: What's the matter? That little Basque girl won't have you? Is that it?

RHYS: I didn't ask her. I'm asking you. Now, what's it going to be? Make up your mind, because I've got to get the hell out of this town. It's ruining my reputation. I can't find anything to drink and I'm asking a pregnant woman to marry me. The next thing you know, I'll be going to church.

ALISON: It's crazy. Where would we live?

RHYS: Wherever my sadistic editor sends me.

ALISON: That's no life for a child.

RHYS: Have you got a better one to offer it?

ALISON: I just don't understand why you'd want to do a thing like this. I don't want any charity from you. Is it because of that other woman named Alison?

RHYS: Yes. Every time I meet a woman named Alison I ask her to marry me. I have seventeen wives named Alison scattered all over the world. Just change your name to Flossie and I'll be gone in a flash. Does it really matter?

ALISON: Yes it matters.

RHYS: I'm forty years old, and I have absolutely nobody, and neither do you.

(Pause.)

ALISON: I'm insane if I do.

RHYS: That's all right. I've always secretly hoped to marry a madwoman, and now I've found one, and her father owns a bar. It's fate. Are you crying again? I wish you wouldn't do that. It's a lot less disturbing when you're just punching me in the nose.

ALISON: Don't you ever cry?

RHYS: I expect I'll learn after I'm married.

ALISON: I can't. I really can't. But thank you for asking.

RHYS: You could do a lot worse.

ALISON: I don't see how.

RHYS: OK. I have no home and very little future. I drink too much, I'm not to be trusted always, and most of my life I've been in love with another woman with your name, and it's true I'm extremely fond of that little Basque girl. On the other hand, it wouldn't be dull. You could see the world. The kid could see the world. It would give your child a father. It would give my life the illusion of purpose. And it would give you somebody to blame all your troubles on.

ALISON: But, Rhys, you don't love me.

RHYS: Let's not make any unnecessary assumptions here.

(Pause. Alison looks at him.)

ALISON: I'll need a few minutes to pack.

(She goes into the back. Rhys goes back over to his drink, picks it up, looks at it, then puts it down again. He stands there.)

THE REDEEMER

Cybèle May

Dramatic

Stewart, a detective with the Allentown police, thirty to fifty; Connie, a psychic and recluse, twenty-five to fifty

> *As the kidnapper plays games with Stewart and Connie, Stewart is driven to the edge. When he returns from a failed attempt to retrieve the boy, Connie confronts him with her knowledge of Stewart's past.*

STEWART: I'm going to kill you.

CONNIE: What?

STEWART: Your gift didn't show it to you?

CONNIE: My God, what is that?

STEWART: Blood, his blood.

CONNIE: What happened?

STEWART: She killed him.

CONNIE: What?

STEWART: There was blood and broken glass everywhere. Enough blood to fill a boy. You made me look like a fool. You whore, you filthy whore.

CONNIE: Who do you think I am?

STEWART: You think I'm lying?

CONNIE: He's not dead. She was singing. She didn't kill him.

STEWART: Yes, she did, she killed all those other boys.

CONNIE: No.

STEWART: It's over. You said we had time. You said we had time and you were wrong.

CONNIE: I would have seen it.

STEWART: Well, you didn't.

CONNIE: What makes you so sure?

STEWART: This!

CONNIE: Maybe it's not his.

STEWART: Shut up! Just shut up, Connie. He's dead. You were supposed to save him. You didn't. It's your fault. You fucked up.

CONNIE: Don't blame me for something that hasn't happened.

STEWART: Didn't you hear me? He's dead. You didn't do enough. This was my case. This was my boy to save and I'm left looking for a body.

CONNIE: Whose boy?

STEWART: Blood, blood everywhere and you're talking about fucking haircuts.

CONNIE: Whose boy?

STEWART: What?

CONNIE: Whose boy to save?

STEWART: I'm warning you. Don't start with me again. Don't you start with me.

CONNIE: Whose boy, Stewart? If everything I've seen about Ryan Thaxter isn't true then what I saw you do to your family can't be true. Now, whose boy are you talking about, Detective?

STEWART: Stop it. I'm not listening to you.

CONNIE: A green car.

STEWART: Stop it.

CONNIE: Foggy.

STEWART: Stop it.

CONNIE: Your wife was putting on her makeup.

STEWART: I'm warn —

CONNIE: Your little boy crouched down behind your seat.

STEWART: Stop.

CONNIE: I saw it. I know.

(He grabs her hair from the back of the neck.)

CONNIE: You killed your wife and boy.

STEWART: It was an accident.

CONNIE: Are you going to kill me, too?

THE REEVES TALE
Don Nigro

Dramatic
John, twenty-seven; Molkin, sixteen

> *In an isolated farmhouse in east Ohio in 1972, something has been
> living in the well and one by one luring everybody out into the strange
> pulsating lights and weird nightmare carnival sounds in the yard.
> The only ones left now are John, a farmhand, and Molkin, whose
> mother Abby has just been unable to resist the impulse to go out in
> the yard and become the latest victim of whatever monstrous thing
> is out there waiting for them. Molkin wants to go and rescue her
> but John knows it's too late, and he is trying to save Molkin.*

MOLKIN: *(Crying and screaming, crawling after Abby.)* MAMA, MAMA,
MAMA.
*(Molkin is about to crawl out the door into the pulsating lights and noises
when John tackles her and pulls her back, slamming the door behind them,
his back against it. Molkin struggles.)*
MOLKIN: No. Let me go. I want my mama. I want my mama.
(John holds her firmly, not letting go.)
MOLKIN: No. No. No. No. No.
(Finally Molkin stops struggling and just cries.)
JOHN: *(Holding her, stroking her hair.)* What you and I are going to do is,
what you and I, you and I are going to — you and I are going to sit
down here and have something to eat.
MOLKIN: I don't want to eat.
JOHN: *(Dragging her over to the table.)* Sit down and eat.
MOLKIN: There's nothing left to eat.
JOHN: *(Retrieving Abby's doughnut off the floor and putting it on a plate.)*
There. Eat this.
MOLKIN: I'm not gonna eat that dirty old thing. It's been on the floor. It's
got hair on it.

JOHN: EAT IT. EAT IT. EAT. *(John sits her down in a chair at the table.)* YOU EAT THIS. NOW. EAT. YUMMY. EAT IT.

(Molkin, sobbing, frightened, and in despair, begins valiantly to try and eat the doughnut.)

JOHN: Don't worry. I have a plan.

MOLKIN: Oh, great. That eases my mind a lot.

JOHN: It's important to have a plan if you're going to achieve ultimate success in any human endeavor.

MOLKIN: Why does everybody keep going away?

JOHN: So I have, unbeknownst to you, been making preparations for just such, just such an ultimate situation as we now find ourselves in. And my plan is — *(John goes over to the cupboard by the sink.)* — my plan is that I've been collecting rope.

(He reaches into the cupboard and pulls out a great deal of rope.)

MOLKIN: You're going away next, I bet.

JOHN: No I'm not.

MOLKIN: You are. You'll run off like everybody else. You'll get tired of me. You won't love me anymore. I know your kind. You're no good. No man is any good. All men are horseshit. That's my philosophy.

JOHN: You should write that down. You might want to submit that to learned philosophical journals. You could teach at Ohio State with a philosophy like that. This rope is full of knots.

(He is trying to untangle the rope.)

MOLKIN: My daddy went away. Pap went away. Alen went away twice. Mama went away. The dog went away. God, I miss old Spot. The cow went away. The circus left town. And now the television set don't work half the time. I think life is tragic.

JOHN: I'm not going anyplace. I'm going to stay right here with you and fight this thing.

MOLKIN: No, you're going to get in that truck and drive off to the Yucatan peninsula. To Tierra Del Fuego. To the Straits of Magellan. Mozambique. Tanganyika. Upper Volta. Lower Volta. Zanzibar. Woonsocket, Rhode Island.

JOHN: I can't drive to Zanzibar in that truck.

MOLKIN: Why not? Did your license expire?

JOHN: Because there's something growing up through the wheels, and the truck's all green and glows, and something plays the radio at night, only the music sounds like it was underwater and backwards.

(Holding a loop of rope in his hand.)

Come over here.

MOLKIN: When you go, I'll be all alone, and the water faucets is gonna suck me right up into the cesspool, I just know it, and it's gonna eat me like it ate Mama and the cow.

JOHN: Come here, Molkin. It's all right. I'm going to take care of everything.

MOLKIN: I don't see why. You got no stake in this. It ain't your house or nothing. You don't have to stay. Nobody stays, anyway. Nobody sticks it out with you to the end. Everybody goes to Mexico. They all go to Mexico. *(For the first time she really focuses on what John has in his hands.)* What are you doing with that rope?

JOHN: Just come over here.

MOLKIN: What do you want with all that rope for?

JOHN: I'm going to help you.

MOLKIN: With a rope? How you gonna help me with a rope? We gonna run off and join the rodeo?

JOHN: Don't worry about it. Just come here.

(Pause.)

MOLKIN: All right.

(Molkin moves toward him cautiously. John pulls out the rocking chair and sits in it.)

JOHN: Sit in my lap.

MOLKIN: Why?

JOHN: Just sit in my lap.

(Pause. Molkin sits in his lap.)

MOLKIN: The cold makes me sleepy but I'm afraid to go to sleep. I'm worried you'll be gone when I wake up. I don't know what I'd do if I had to be here all alone. *(Noises from outside.)* I'm scared.

JOHN: Don't be scared.

MOLKIN: Well, talk to me.

JOHN: *(Beginning to wrap the rope around them, tying them in the chair.)* What about?

MOLKIN: I don't know. Television. Did they have television when you were my age?

JOHN: Yes, believe it or not, they did.

MOLKIN: Really? Way back then?

JOHN: It was primitive.

MOLKIN: You mean like black and white?

JOHN: Yes.

MOLKIN: That must have been awful for you.

JOHN: No. It was very nice.

(As he speaks, the lights from outside grow more like television light, and he gently coils the rope around them, tying them to the chair.)

JOHN: We lived in Arizona, see, and at night I'd sit by myself in a big dark room, right in front of this square, yellow television set, and eat potato chips and drink Pepsi Cola out of great long bottles and watch *Rawhide*.

MOLKIN: That sounds dirty. Was it dirty?

JOHN: No, it was about cowboys. They took these herds of cows from some-place to someplace, I don't know, Kansas, I think, and they were al-ways roping these cows and riding around on the prairie.

(As John continues to loop more and more coils of rope around them, the warped sounds of deranged cows come wafting in and the light grows in-creasingly ominous.)

Mr. Favor was the trail boss. He was sorta like God, lost his temper a lot and brooded, but he was OK, deep down, you see, and he had this big, dumb, gangly sort of a kid who was his ramrod.

MOLKIN: You sure it wasn't dirty?

JOHN: No, it was Clint Eastwood.

MOLKIN: Are you making this up?

JOHN: I swear. And they'd come upon wonderful things in the night, lights in the middle of nowhere and gypsy wagons in the dark with calliopes that played and rolled along with nobody to drive them.

(Demented carnival music with animal chorus.)

MOLKIN: Where were they taking these cows?

JOHN: I don't know. Slaughterhouse, I guess.

MOLKIN: Poor cows.

(Deranged cow noises.)

JOHN: And also there was Secret Agent John Drake, who was very cool and funny and had a wicked voice like a knife, and sad, cold eyes. He was trapped, see, in this system he hated. He didn't know half the time why he was even doing what he was doing, didn't belong to anyplace or anything, couldn't touch things, was separated from all touch, cold. Taking on grotesque identities. Making investigations in the dark. It was like a series of black and white and gray coded messages from God. If you could just break the code, you could understand. Not escape, maybe, because they were all trapped in that square yellow box, but at least begin to comprehend a part of the true nature of, the geography of, the darkness that was devouring you.

MOLKIN: I'm gettin' scared again.

JOHN: And Ed Sullivan, he was this man who moved sort of like a zombie, and he had an Italian mouse he would talk to, and people that spinned plates on sticks, and a woman that rode a unicycle with bare buttocks, and two guys with slicked down hair that sang *Santa Lucia* with a cello, and the Great Grok, who did an act with a mannequin, and Ben Blue who danced around a chair, and Senor Wences, who talked to his hand. He drew a face on his hand with lipstick and put a wig on it and hung a little suit with legs from it and talked to his hand, and it talked back to him. It was a little boy named Johnny. And he also had a head that lived in a box, and he'd open the box and ask the head if it was all right, and the head would say — *(Very deep voice, Spanish accent.)* All right. *(Normal voice.)* And he'd close the box and ask his hand if it was all right, and the hand would say — *(Falsetto, Spanish accent.)* All right. *(Normal voice.)* And he'd tell the hand that he was a good boy, and not to be afraid, and the hand would say — *(Falsetto, Spanish accent.)* I am not afraid.

(Pause. Relative quiet from outside, just a faint buzzing.)

MOLKIN: The noise went away. Maybe it's gone. Do you think it's gone?

JOHN: Maybe.

MOLKIN: I was thinkin' how nice it might be to die, because when you die, you never got to have sex again. God, Johnny, you don't think Hell is having to have sex all the time, do you? Or even worse, Heaven. That'd be awful, with everybody playin' on harps and eatin' angel food cake and watchin' you do it and all.

JOHN: I don't think death is like that. I think it's more like the *Ed Sullivan Show*. Everybody gets a chance to do their own particular act, no matter how weird it is.

MOLKIN: That would be nice. *(Pause.)* You won't go away from me, will you, Johnny? Promise me you won't ever go away from me.

JOHN: Not me. I live here. This is where I belong. This is my home. This is the inside of my own personal television set. And I am not afraid. Are you afraid?

MOLKIN: Not very. Not so much.

JOHN: Good. All right?

MOLKIN: All right.

(John ties one final knot. Molkin cuddles against him and closes her eyes. Then a sudden, horrible blast of noise and lights hits them, and the lights go out.)

THE RUBY SUNRISE

Rinne Groff

Dramatic
Ruby, late teens; Henry, not much older

> *Ruby has run away from home and is staying with her aunt at her farm. She is something of a technological genius, and she is working on a project in her aunt's barn — she's very close to inventing what will some day be known as "television" (the scene takes place in the 1930s). Henry is a boarder with her aunt. He may be sweet on Ruby, but she has no time for any of that. She's determined to invent television.*

> *The Barn. Ruby is working on her television. Connecting wires in a circuit. Henry enters. He stands by the barn door for a moment before Ruby sees him.*

RUBY: Hey. I thought you were at the library.

HENRY: I was.

RUBY: Don't you have an exam tomorrow?

HENRY: Yeah.

RUBY: Well, Mr. Dean's List, what are you doing back here?

HENRY: Quit.

RUBY: What?

HENRY: Quit messing with the wires for once.

(She looks up from her equipment.)

RUBY: What happened to you?

HENRY: I took a break. When I was studying. I went to the newspapers.

RUBY: OK.

HENRY: They had the *Indianapolis Ledger.*

RUBY: OK, the *Indianapolis Ledger.*

HENRY: Ruby, they already did it.

RUBY: Did what?

HENRY: What you're doing. It's done.

RUBY: Nobody's doing what I'm doing.

HENRY: You're wrong.

(He pulls out a piece of paper.)

HENRY: I wrote it down on account of how I knew you wouldn't trust my word. *(Reading.)* Far-off Speakers Seen as Well as Heard in New York City in a Test of Television.

RUBY: What are you talking about?

HENRY: *(Still reading.)* Like a Photo Come to Life. Hoover's Face Plainly Imaged as He Speaks in Washington. *(Looking up.)* The American Telegraph and Telephone Company, they did it. The paper explained how and everything. *(Reading.)* Dots of light are put together at a rate of 45,000 a second . . . *(Looking up.)* And like that. I couldn't write it all down. I'll take you tomorrow. It seems this fellow Dr. Ives . . .

RUBY: Who?

HENRY: Ives, he's a Doctor. *(From the paper.)* And R.C. Mathes . . .

(Ruby begins to speak.)

HENRY: Or Maths. Matheez, I guess. Why are you laughing?

(Ruby goes back to her equipment.)

RUBY: Henry, it doesn't matter.

HENRY: They did it. They made a Television. It's over.

RUBY: Ives and Gray are still working with spinning wooden disks. I read their article eight months ago. It's nothing. Bet the picture was for diddly-squat. What was it: two inches wide?

HENRY: Two by three, it said.

RUBY: Inches. Inches, Henry. Would you go to the the-ater if it was two inches big?

HENRY: By three. And they showed it on a bigger screen, too.

RUBY: But it must've looked like hell, all white spots and smudges.

HENRY: It said it was a little unclear.

RUBY: Even they admit that to get a four by four inch picture, they're gonna need a six-foot diameter disk. You want a six-foot thing spinning in your living room?

HENRY: But they beat you. You can stop now.

RUBY: I'm not making this up. American Telegraph is trying to do it me-chanically.

HENRY: The *Indianapolis Ledger* says . . .

RUBY: The *Indianapolis Ledger*, the *Indianapolis Ledger*, I can say it, too; it doesn't make it holy. The picture is for squat. I don't need the local paper to tell me that. Why don't you have the guts to say that you don't think I can do it, instead of parading some trash piece of paper like it's the News that's doubting me instead of you.

HENRY: Who the hell gets you those tubes, that wire? For crying out loud, every piece of crap in here came from me whether I bought it or stole it, sorry, "borrowed" it. I did all that.

RUBY: You want it back? You want your share of the investment?

HENRY: Aww, stop it.

RUBY: I buy you out, here and now, you're bought out, I'll pay you back every cent as soon as I file and my patent clears. And when people say my name, you'll be sorry then.

HENRY: Nobody's gonna be saying your name.

RUBY: What do you know? How could I expect you to understand?

HENRY: That phony contraption isn't ever gonna do what you say.

RUBY: And they laughed at Marconi, too.

HENRY: It's too late. Admit it, Ruby. What will it take for you to quit this nonsense?

RUBY: Ignorant cattle farmer.

HENRY: Crazy Girl from Kokomo.

(For a moment Ruby stops her work, stops moving.)

RUBY: Get out.

HENRY: I'm sorry.

RUBY: Get out of my laboratory. I'm working. I don't need any of you.

(She goes back to adjusting the wires.)

HENRY: Miss Haver let it slip one night. I'm sorry.

RUBY: I'm working, I said.

HENRY: Put down the wires for a minute. Your aunt told me lots of things. I was waiting for you to come clean yourself.

RUBY: Don't come one step closer.

HENRY: I love you. I want to take care of you.

RUBY: I said, stop.

HENRY: What's wrong with that? That's normal.

RUBY: I'm not hearing a thing you're saying.

HENRY: I know the truth about your daddy. I know he's coming here. Soon.

RUBY: I'm not listening, I said.

HENRY: I'm saying I'll marry you.

> *(Suddenly, Ruby screams out in pain as she is thrown across the barn with an electrical shock. She slams into the floor. The entire circuit of the TV system sizzles and fumes. The electric lights pop out. Ruby's body is shaking. Henry rushes to her.)*

HENRY: Are you OK? Ruby, honey, are you OK?

RUBY: My baby.

> *(He looks at her, realizing what she's said.)*

HENRY: Oh my God.

THE RUBY SUNRISE
Rinne Groff

Dramatic
Tad, late twenties to thirties; Elizabeth, twenties

> *Tad is a TV writer whose latest project is a drama about a teenaged girl's attempt to invent what will become television. This part of the play takes place in a TV studio during the heyday of live TV drama in the 1950s. Elizabeth, a gifted Broadway stage actress, was hired to play the teenaged inventor, but then fired because her name turned up on the infamous "blacklist." Her career over, she visits the studio, where she meets the writer of what would have been her Breakthrough Role.*

> *(A simply dressed young woman [Elizabeth Hunter] stands on the empty Kitchen/Barn set. She looks around. Tad enters. He seems shocked by the sight of her. He watches her. Finally she notices him.)*

ELIZABETH: I'm sorry; I was only looking around; I'm just leaving.

TAD: No, it's OK.

> *(Tad stares at her.)*

ELIZABETH: Are you Security?

TAD: No.

ELIZABETH: Do I know you?

TAD: No. I don't think so. I mean I recognize you. You're an actress.

ELIZABETH: Guilty as charged. Are you involved in this production?

TAD: No. Are you?

ELIZABETH: No. No.

TAD: What are you doing here then?

ELIZABETH: You're sure you're not Security?

TAD: I hate security.

ELIZABETH: Do you know Martin Marcus?

TAD: The producer?

ELIZABETH: He tried to get me some extra work on the variety they're shooting upstairs. I was literally going to be a pair of legs in a crowd scene. You wouldn't even see my profile. But some agency guy spotted me. "Is that Liz Hunter? Get her out of here." I said, "No, I'm nobody, just a brunette trying to earn a nickel." "Get her out of here."

TAD: They're maniacs.

ELIZABETH: I think "maniac" is generous.

TAD: Can I have your autograph?

ELIZABETH: My autograph?

TAD: I saw you in that show at the Lyceum. You're tremendous.

ELIZABETH: I don't think the autograph will be worth much.

TAD: That can't be true; you're a rising star.

ELIZABETH: I'll let you in on a little secret; my career is officially over. I guess I learned that today.

TAD: You were slated to perform on this set?

ELIZABETH: Slated? I don't know. I read the first act.

TAD: What was it about?

ELIZABETH: Despair. I mean, persistence.

TAD: Huh.

ELIZABETH: "It happened just like this. I was on the mower, riding it down the field, each row, all those straight, straight lines. My thoughts, as usual, weren't on farming; I was building something else in my mind. And right then, as the rein slipped from my hand . . . Eureka! I figured it out. You gotta magnetically deflect electrons across the Television screen in the same way you plow a field. Back and forth. Line by line. Rows and rows and rows, just like the field. This is the twentieth century. And it's time to romance the electron."

TAD: You must have an amazing memory.

ELIZABETH: It's a curse.

TAD: It seems like you would have nailed the part.

ELIZABETH: The world will never know. You still want that signature?

TAD: *(Searching.)* I don't have any paper.

ELIZABETH: A writer without paper.

TAD: How'd you know I'm a writer?

ELIZABETH: A certain smell: over-worked and under-appreciated.
(Going in her bag.)

I've got a publicity photo in here somewhere; might as well use them up. How would that suit you?

TAD: That would be amazing.

ELIZABETH: Who should I make it out to?

TAD: Mitch.

ELIZABETH: Just Mitch?

TAD: Mitch is good.

(She writes on the picture.)

TAD: I don't believe your career is over. You're too talented; it can't be right.

ELIZABETH: I didn't say it was right; I said it was over.

(She holds the picture out to him. He hesitates.)

ELIZABETH: What's wrong?

TAD: My name is Tad Rose, and I'm sorry.

ELIZABETH: You didn't seem like a Mitch.

TAD: You deserved better. Maybe if I had been more brave . . .

ELIZABETH: That was pretty brave; confessing. Don't you want to read what I wrote?

TAD: What?

ELIZABETH: My autograph.

(He takes it and reads.)

TAD: Dear Mr. Rose, May God Forgive Us All.

ELIZABETH: I had such dreams. New York City. I was going to be the best they'd ever seen.

TAD: You could testify. They'd welcome you back. You were young and made a big mistake. Sign right here.

ELIZABETH: I want a career, I also need to sleep at night.

TAD: I will never come close to being what you are.

ELIZABETH: It's funny. Growing up, they called me Scaredy-Cat Lizzie. How strange when it comes down to it, and you turn out to be a little bit brave. It's such a pain in the ass.

TAD: I can't get you back on the show.

ELIZABETH: I hope you don't expect me to say, Oh, it's all right, don't even try.

TAD: No.

ELIZABETH: Maybe when someone calls your number, you'll surprise yourself, too.

TAD: I know I'm not a hero.

ELIZABETH: You're lucky.

Will you save my picture?

TAD: I will. Of course, I will.

ELIZABETH: No, I mean it, Mr. Rose. Save that picture.

SANS-CULOTTES IN THE PROMISED LAND

Kirsten Greenidge

Dramatic
Carol and Greg (probably midthirties)

> *Carol and Greg are a very successful, upwardly mobile, black couple with an eight-year-old daughter. Greg is something of a philanderer. Carol is a control freak.*

CAROL: Everyone thinks we multiply like rabbits and you went and proved them right.

GREG: This isn't my fault, Carol, if you want to blame anyone blame Carrmel. I couldn't tell you before because she . . . She's very threatening, Carol. Or she can be. To me. But I've changed. So I can tell you now that Carrmel's been poking holes in your personal —

CAROL: Don't bring Carrmel into this.

GREG: She told me herself. You can ask her —

CAROL: I'm not going to ask our housekeeper why I got pregnant.

GREG: Ask how: She knows *how.*

CAROL: And these are holes you've actually seen? Actually laid eyes on?

GREG: Well, no, but she had that thing in her hand, why else would she have that thing in her hand?

CAROL: Did you ask to see these holes? I would have wanted evidence.

GREG: She *showed* me the evidence.

CAROL: But you didn't see any holes, did you? Carrmel will say anything to get attention, Greg. You shouldn't let her get to you and you certainly shouldn't indulge her by taking her so seriously. This baby is not her fault: *You're* never careful. Do I have to remind you how we got our first one?

GREG: We wouldn't have to worry about being careful if it weren't for Carrmel —

CAROL: Honestly I don't even know when I last used that thing anyway. It's not like we often —. I always figured if something happened I'd have it taken care of —

GREG: Taken care of?

CAROL: We don't deserve another baby. What on earth would we do with it? We've always agreed Greta is enough.

GREG: Is enough.

CAROL: Especially since I've already ruined her: Have you *seen* her? She's dirty.

GREG: We'll give her a bath, how hard can it be?

CAROL: I tried that. I got close enough to her because she'd asked me to but I couldn't make it to the tub so I licked a little corner of my finger, like I think I see mothers on the subway do, like this? And I rubbed my finger around in a circle and even though it was spit and not water and soap she appreciated it. She looked at me and kind of smiled a little. I smiled a little too. And then I felt it. A knot taking all my energy, making it too hard to keep my finger moving. Only a certain kind of woman hands her energy away to other people, little people. I'm not that kind.

GREG: I have news that might make things better.

CAROL: *(Wryly.)* You're pregnant?

GREG: I have a client, well, almost a client. I think it's going to work out. I can feel it. This one's special —

CAROL: Thank God I provide or Greta'd be out in the street, going to public school, taking lessons from amateurs at the Y and being a latch key child, if it were left to you.

GREG: That's not fair, Carol. You know how hard I try. I show people my designs and they snicker. Why don't they hire me?

CAROL: Your work is good.

GREG: My last job was for that bank and they didn't even use half the stuff I made.

CAROL: It's just a little/ethnic.

GREG: Ethnic. That's what they say, I know that's what they always say, but I think I have imagination. I have vision. Except no one will give me a chance —

CAROL: Don't bring that black man stuff around me. It's not you, it's the work. You're building America, Greg, not Timbuktu. Remember that. We're leaders. We're pioneers. We came from nothing and now look. Look at how far we've come. Which is exactly why my "situation" must be *temporary*. What will people think if it seems like we can't keep our legs together and keep focused, really focused, on our role in this world?

GREG: But it there's a baby involved we should readjust, reevaluate. . . . Maybe move to a smaller —

CAROL: I don't know why I even bother explaining these things to you, it's not like you care about them.

GREG: I do —

CAROL: It's not like you work for them, bleed for them, like I do.

GREG: Now, that's not fair —

CAROL: I bleed for them, all by myself. While you stay safe and whole in here, while you dally in your "art" and your "heritage," I bleed. Reevaluate. Ha. Some of us don't have that luxury, Greg. Some of us realize this is America and you don't get anywhere special if you don't pay attention, if you don't know you've got to be the very best and expect the very best every single minute of every single day. And once you let your guard down you may as well curl up and die because that's not who gets anywhere in this country, Greg. We're pioneers. Why can't you understand that?

GREG: Maybe . . . maybe when we were planning, way back, maybe we were wrong. Maybe we didn't know it'd take so much of us —

CAROL: Everything is maybe with you. Even me. Even this marriage. Don't think I've forgotten. How your fingers go walking, how you —

GREG: Stop.

CAROL: — you and those girls —

GREG: It was once. It was five girls ago and it was *once*.

CAROL: Because of me, because of me, poof, easy as —

GREG: You want to know what it was, Carol? It was little hills of skin and bone that stick out of her where normal people keep their arms and hands attached. It was knowing those little hills weren't locked away

in an office or attached to a phone. It was knowing they were roam-
ing free around me, that I might accidentally bump into them, that
maybe —

CAROL: Everything is maybe with you. It was only once because you probably couldn't make it past maybe to more than once. Your whole life
is maybe, that's your problem.

THE STANWAY CASE
Sam Bobrick

Comic
Maura and Scott, thirties

> *Maura and Scott, jurors on a very unusual court case, have struck
> up a romantic relationship.*

> *Early evening. The front door opens and Maura and Scott enter.
> Scott carries a bag of groceries that contain take-out food. Maura
> turns on the lights and takes the bag from Scott.*

SCOTT: I'm really glad we decided to bring food up. After sitting all day
long in that courtroom, I'm not sure I could have handled sitting in
a restaurant for any length of time.

MAURA: I don't remember ever being so drained. *(Opens kitchen doors, places
bag on the counter and begins removing containers of food and a bottle
of wine.)*

SCOTT: I did everything I could to keep from nodding off.

MAURA: Really? I don't know why. I found the day absolutely riveting.

SCOTT: My fatigue was not from the trial. It came from being awakened
at three in the morning and told to go home.

MAURA: Well, I knew you wouldn't want to show up in court wearing the
exact same clothes you had on the day before. We certainly don't want
to start anyone talking. Maybe after we adjourned you should have
gone straight home and to bed.

SCOTT: How could I do that? If you recall, I had a hot date tonight. Actually, I'm starting to get a second wind. *(From behind he tries to nuz-
zle his cheek against hers.)* It could be from being close to you.

MAURA: That's sweet. *(Maura moves away, continuing to set up their dinner on the coffee table.)* You know what I find most fascinating about
this trial? Stanway himself. His utter lack of emotions. He just sits
there expressionless. Even during the detailed and gory way the pros-
ecuting attorney described how he killed her.

SCOTT: Allegedly killed her.

MAURA: Yes, OK. Allegedly killed her. Anyway, I would think that if he really was innocent, this ordeal he's now going through would have to be a total nightmare for him. If he really was innocent you'd think there would be some expression of indignation or horror during the relating of the incident. My God, his wife is horribly bludgeoned to death and every time it's brought up, he just sits there showing absolutely nothing. No outrage, no pain, no grief, nothing. I find it almost impossible to believe that this is the behavior of an innocent man.

SCOTT: Time is a great healer. Don't forget he's been under arrest and awaiting trial for several months. I'm sure he's well aware of all the gory details and he's probably already dealt with that. Maybe if he was guilty he would put on the kind of show you think he should put on.

MAURA: I guess I'm not convinced he's at all remorseful. If I were in his shoes I would find this detached attitude very difficult to maintain no matter how much time has passed.

SCOTT: Fortunately I've never met a murderer so I wouldn't know how they behave or what goes through their minds. What about you? Have you ever met a murderer?

MAURA: Met one? No. Not that I know of. Anyway, what's the point you're trying to make?

SCOTT: No point. I'm just trying to get you to take a deep breath and chill out a little. There's still a lot that needs to be revealed about the case. It's just the second day. No one needs to come to any decision now. There's plenty of time.

MAURA: I know, you're right.

SCOTT: Thank you.

MAURA: But I also know I'm right about him doing it. I'll tell you what I also found fascinating. That so many of his friends were so willing to testify against him.

SCOTT: They weren't really testifying against him. They were simply verifying what seemed to be common knowledge, that his wife had a lover and he wasn't very happy about it.

MAURA: *(As she goes about dishing out food into plates.)* Pointing to all the reasons for his killing her. Jealousy, rage, betrayal.

SCOTT: My God, you've all but picked out the date this poor guy goes to the gas chamber, haven't you?

MAURA: No. Of course not. I said I could be fair and I will be. I'm simply going over what I was impressed by.

SCOTT: They also said that he was very much in love with her. Desperately in love with her.

MAURA: Which only adds fuel to the fire.

SCOTT: Pointing to a crime of passion if anything.

MAURA: Whatever the reason was, it's still murder. God, I still feel sick when I think of the photos they made us look at. Her skull smashed to bits by that brick and all that blood. All that horrible blood. You want to open the wine? There's a corkscrew in the desk drawer.

SCOTT: Oh, sure.

(Maura sets out two wine glasses on the coffee table. During the following Scott goes to the desk.)

SCOTT: *(Continuing.)* That bothered me. Why a brick? He owned a gun. And there were plenty of knives around the house. Why a brick that obviously came from outside the house?

MAURA: I don't think it's necessary for us to concern ourselves over the way he chose to kill her. Our job is simply a case of did he or didn't he and unfortunately I think he did.

SCOTT: I know. But it just seems too easy. I mean if a guy is going to kill someone and then plead innocent, why would he make it so easy to convict him?

MAURA: That's true. On the other hand, it's probably the first time he's killed someone. Maybe next time he'll be more professional.

(Scott turns to her. They look at each other for a beat.)

SCOTT: You're cute, you know that? You are very very cute . . . when you let yourself be.

MAURA: Am I?

SCOTT: Very. *(He is about to open the desk drawer when a folder on top of the desk catches his eye. He picks it up and opens it.)* What's this? "The Stanway Case." You're keeping a file?

MAURA: *(Going to him.)* Well, I'm just starting to. I was hoping the case might make a good book. Possibly even a play. At this point I'm not exactly sure.

SCOTT: You're a writer?

MAURA: I'd like to think I am. That's another reason why I came to New York. It seems unless you've spent some time on the East Coast, no one really takes what you write very seriously.

SCOTT: Then you've been published?

MAURA: Well, no, not yet, which is a little troubling because I'm not sure it's really ethical to call yourself a writer until one's been published. It's a bit of a thin line.

SCOTT: Well, maybe this Stanway case will do the trick. *(Leafs through pages.)* You've already got a bunch of notes. I'm impressed, especially since it's only the second day of the trail. When did you find time to start this?

MAURA: Early this morning. After you left, I jotted down some things that I thought were important. Anyway, it's not for anyone's eyes yet. *(Taking the folder from Scott, she places it in a desk drawer.)*

SCOTT: You've got to promise to let me read it when you finish, although I guess I'll know how it ends, won't I?

MAURA: Maybe. *(She then takes out the corkscrew from the desk drawer and hands it to Scott.)* Here you are. The corkscrew. I don't know why I keep it in the desk.

SCOTT: Why not? It's near the wine rack. It makes sense. *(He takes the bottle of wine from the kitchen counter and opens it.)*

SCOTT: *(Continuing.)* Anyway, let's forget the case tonight, OK? Let's talk about other things. Let's talk about last night. It was pretty amazing, wasn't it? I mean for me, anyway. How was it for you? I know this is a little late to be asking that but better late than never. By the way, is that part going to be in your book? It could help sales. *(He puts the corkscrew back in the drawer, crosses to coffee table and pours two glasses of wine.)*

MAURA: *(A beat.)* I admire you. I really do. You are approaching this trial in such a fair and logical manner. And in the end I suppose I will too, but right now, cut and dry, the best I can say is Stanway is guilty as sin. *(She returns to sofa.)*

SCOTT: You don't give an inch, do you?

MAURA: At times I have been accused of having somewhat of a stubborn streak.

SCOTT: Look, what if we make a pact, put it in writing and sign it? When we leave the jury room, we leave the case there too. Does that sound reasonable?

MAURA: You are asking me to suppress my feelings.

SCOTT: *(Sits next to Maura.)* I'm asking you to obey the judge and the law. I think at the end of the day we need to leave it all in the courtroom.

MAURA: It seems I'm obviously more affected by this trial than you. Maybe it's because I'm a woman. We seem to be more sensitive in some areas than our male counterparts.

SCOTT: Come on, Maura. You know just as well as I do that's pure bullshit.

MAURA: Well, I think we do.

SCOTT: *(Slightly irritated.)* Think, think, think. Maybe that's your problem. Maybe you need to concentrate on what you hear, not what you think.

MAURA: *(Playfully.)* OK, I'll buy that and so far everything I've heard seems to point to him and I doubt very much that he's going to get away with it and I don't see how anyone on that jury in their right mind can see it any other way.

SCOTT: God, you're a friggin' handful, aren't you? *(Hands a wine glass to Maura and then offers a toast.)* Well, here's to us.

MAURA: No. "To you and me," please. I'm not ready for "us" just yet.

SCOTT: Will that make you more comfortable?

MAURA: For now it would.

SCOTT: "To you and me."

(The lighting changes to surreal.)

MAURA: *(Rising, upset.)* I need to know where you stand, Scott. I need to know why the hell you even think there's a possibility that Stanway didn't do it. Trust me. He's an abusive, controlling pig. I know that kind of man. He would rather see his wife dead than lose her. I . . . I can't talk to you about this anymore. Maybe I need to be alone.

SCOTT: Look, get a grip. We've got something special here, you and I. Why can't you see that? I want to keep this relationship going and no matter what you say it is now a relationship.

MAURA: No it isn't. At best it's an affair and frankly one I'd now like to reconsider.

(Maura sits. She regains her composure. The lighting changes back to normal. Scott is unaware of the surreal moment.)

SCOTT: *(Repeating his toast.)* "To you and me."

(They clink glasses together and drink.)

MAURA: What did you mean when you said I'm cute when I let myself be?

SCOTT: I meant that you have the ability to be very cute, actually bordering on adorable, when you let your guard down a bit. When you don't seem to be . . . hiding things.

MAURA: Hiding things? How did you arrive at that? I think I've been very open.

SCOTT: Yes. About the case. But other than that you just seem so damn cautious about everything else. I feel you've built some kind of a wall around you and I'm wondering at what point do I get let in because I'd really like to be.

MAURA: Yes. I . . . I know that.

SCOTT: Maybe after the trial. Maybe that's when you'll feel more at ease with our situation. God, even today in court, you seemed to go out of your way to avoid any hint of intimacy between us. You wouldn't sit next to me at lunch and every break we took you seemed to disappear somewhere. Actually, I felt a little rejected.

(They begin to eat.)

MAURA: I'm sorry but I didn't want anyone getting any ideas.

SCOTT: That we're involved with one another? I don't see anything wrong with that since the fact seems to be that we are.

MAURA: Well, it doesn't seem appropriate. I mean not so soon.

SCOTT: I think that's the magic of the situation. That it was so soon. And the fact that I'm here for a second night and drinking wine, that should tell you something. Besides, I would hate knowing I was nothing more than a one-night stand. You're not sorry about last night, are you?

MAURA: Maybe a little.

SCOTT: Oh.

MAURA: Actually, a lot.

SCOTT: Because we had sex on our first night?

MAURA: It's not something a woman is usually proud of.

SCOTT: Yes, but on the other hand it's something a man is, so the two things sort of balance each other out. Anyway, if you want some sort of stronger commitment on my part, I'm more than willing.

MAURA: No. I don't need that.

SCOTT: Maybe I do.

MAURA: Look, it's much too soon to make what happened last night more important than what it was.

SCOTT: And what do you think it was?

MAURA: It was simply two people who didn't want to be alone at that particular point in time.

SCOTT: You need to know this about me, Maura. I'm very self-sufficient when I need to be. I have no trouble spending my nights alone even though I don't particularly like it. I wanted to be with you because I wanted to be with you. It had nothing to do with not wanting to be alone or just wanting to have sex. It was strictly you, Maura. I wanted to be with you.

MAURA: Scott, doesn't it bother you that I seem to be acting so unreasonable about Stanway?

SCOTT: It concerns me. It doesn't bother me.

MAURA: He did kill her, you know. He definitely did kill her.

SCOTT: So what?

(He kisses her.)

STONE COLD DEAD SERIOUS

Adam Rapp

Dramatic
Wynne and Shaylee, teens

> *Wynne and Shaylee are brother and sister. She is a runaway, re-cently returned home. He is a video game whiz.*

> *The knob to the front door is jiggled. The failure of keys. Cursing from a young woman can be heard. Moments later Shaylee can be seen peering in through the living room window. The window is lifted, she quietly crawls through. She is seventeen, pretty but sickly looking. She wears old jogging pants rolled down at the waist, old running shoes. She carries a bag that contains the few fragmented parts of her life. She looks around the living room, runs upstairs, comes back down. Perhaps she limps a bit. She studies the labels on the pill bottles. She opens the bottles, takes a few, chases with Old Style dregs. She stares at the block of knives, removes a small par-ing knife, puts it in her bag. She crosses to the living room shelves and starts to rummage through stuff, looking for money, anything valuable, puts things in her bag. Wynne enters, watches her. After a moment, Shaylee turns, stands. They are frozen.*

SHAYLEE: Hey.

WYNNE: Hey.

SHAYLEE: What's up?

WYNNE: Nothin'.

> *(He looks around to see what she's taken.)*

SHAYLEE: What?

WYNNE: What?

SHAYLEE: So gimme a hug, ya little dick.

> *(He crosses to her. They hug. She goes for his pocket.)*

SHAYLEE: Lend me five bucks.

WYNNE: No.

SHAYLEE: *(Digging in.)* Why not?

WYNNE: Cause I don't got it.

SHAYLEE: *(Really digging in now.)* Yes you do, Mr. Computer Fixer. Five fuckin' bucks, man!

(Wynne pushes her away. Some loose change falls out of his pocket. Shaylee desperately goes after the scattered change.)

SHAYLEE: Smells like shit in here.

WYNNE: Where you been staying?

SHAYLEE: At the Y.

WYNNE: What Y?

SHAYLEE: The one in Franklin Park.

WYNNE: Who's payin' for it?

SHAYLEE: This guy Ed.

WYNNE: Ed who?

SHAYLEE: Just Ed. I met him near the candy machines.

WYNNE: Ma sees you here she'll call the cops.

SHAYLEE: So?

WYNNE: You're like shakin'.

SHAYLEE: *(Sitting.)* No I ain't.

WYNNE: You look like shit.

SHAYLEE: You look like a geek.

WYNNE: You ain't eatin' are you?

SHAYLEE: I eat.

WYNNE: You're so skinny.

SHAYLEE: I just ate somethin' the other day.

WYNNE: What, you chewed an aspirin, drank some nose spray?

SHAYLEE: I ate a banana.

(Wynne grabs the paper sack from under the coffee table.)

SHAYLEE: What's in the bag?

WYNNE: Nothin'.

SHAYLEE: *(Mocking.)* Nothin'.

WYNNE: It's a Taser gun.

(He takes it out, shows it to her.)

SHAYLEE: Where'd you get it?

WYNNE: From this guy Palumbo knows in Libertyville.

SHAYLEE: What's it for?

WYNNE: Tasering. Ever been Tasered?

SHAYLEE: No. Why, you wanna Taser me?

WYNNE: No. It's for protection.

SHAYLEE: How much was it?

WYNNE: I scored it for eighty bucks. They go for two hundred on the black market.

(He puts it in his back pocket. Shaylee pulls out a small box that contains many feeble cigarette butts, lights one, smokes.)

WYNNE: When'd you start smokin'?

SHAYLEE: I don't know. At some point I guess. Where's Ma been hidin' her cigarettes?

WYNNE: She quit.

SHAYLEE: Bullshit.

WYNNE: She did. Last month. She used the patch.

SHAYLEE: *(Quickly rising, crossing to credenza behind the sofa, looting again.)* Fuckin' over-the-counter bitch.

WYNNE: Palumbo saw you in Joliet. He said you were on the casino boat and that you were with some rich Iranian dude who was wearin' a popcorn bucket on his head.

SHAYLEE: His name's Amir and it's called a fez. He's Moroccan.

WYNNE: Palumbo said you were playin' slots.

SHAYLEE: *(Crossing back to the sofa, sitting, trying to smoke.)* Amir was payin', I was pullin'.

WYNNE: Palumbo said he tried talkin to you but you kept sayin' you didn't know him and that your name was Katrina.

SHAYLEE: I guess I was Katrina that night.

WYNNE: He said you were dressed like a whore.

SHAYLEE: Little wop wouldn't know a whore if one walked up and spit on him.

WYNNE: He said you had so much makeup on you looked dead.

SHAYLEE: Maybe I am.

WYNNE: I love you, Shaylee.

SHAYLEE: Good. Gimme five bucks.

WYNNE: You should talk to Ma. Give her a call.

SHAYLEE: Fuck that bitch.

WYNNE: If you get your shit together she'd prolly let you come home.

SHAYLEE: I don't wanna get my shit together.

WYNNE: Pop misses you.

SHAYLEE: So?

WYNNE: He talks about you all the time. The other day he was in your closet holdin your nightgown.

SHAYLEE: Boo-hoo-hoo, what a fuckin' drag, huh?

WYNNE: They kept your room just like it was. Your runnin' trophies and everything.

SHAYLEE: Tell 'em to rent it out, board it up, have a fuckin' garage sale.
(A beat.)

WYNNE: I'm going to New York.

SHAYLEE: For what?

WYNNE: This video game competition. I'm one of the three finalists. If I win I get a shitloada money. I'll give you some. I could send it to you at the Y in Franklin Park. You could go to that place in Michigan and get clean. That place with all the maple trees.

SHAYLEE: Gimme five bucks I'll show you my pussy. *(Pushing the front of her jogging pants down.)* See?
(Wynne steps away, crosses to the kitchen. After a silence:)

SHAYLEE: Drinkin' alone, huh?

WYNNE: That's Pop.

SHAYLEE: Where is he?

WYNNE: In the tub.

SHAYLEE: What's he doin' home?

WYNNE: He hurt his back.

SHAYLEE: Last time I was here I saw his dick. I was hidin' in the shower. He walked in and took a piss. It looked like a mushroom. Like something that gets left in a salad bowl.
      What happened to his back?

WYNNE: He herniated a disc.

SHAYLEE: Stupid fuck. How'd he do that?

WYNNE: Bendin' over backwards glazin' a window. He's s'posed to have an operation to fuse his vertebrae but we can't afford it. He gets shooting pains down his legs. It fucks him up pretty bad. He shits his pants, has to wear diapers.

SHAYLEE: Is he gettin workmen's comp?

WYNNE: Yeah.

SHAYLEE: You know where he keeps his money?

WYNNE: Ma keeps it.

SHAYLEE: Where?

WYNNE: In her music box. But it's mostly checks.

SHAYLEE: *(Starting for the stairs.)* I can cash checks.

WYNNE: Don't take too many.

SHAYLEE: I'll take whatever I please.

WYNNE: Fine! Fuck it!

(She stops halfway up the stairs, sits. Wynne fiddles with his Taser gun.)

SHAYLEE: Guess what?

WYNNE: What.

SHAYLEE: I got hepatitis. My armpits are yellow, wanna see?

WYNNE: No.

SHAYLEE: I fucked this Chink in the back of the 7-Eleven in Elk Grove. I think he gave it to me. His dick stunk like shit. I'm gonna buy a gun, hunt the fucker down. Stick it up his ass and pull the trigger . . . Got a girlfriend?

WYNNE: Sorta.

SHAYLEE: Who?

WYNNE: She's one of the three finalists.

SHAYLEE: What's her name?

WYNNE: Why?

SHAYLEE: Cause I'm jealous.

WYNNE: It's Sharice.

SHAYLEE: She a nigger?

WYNNE: I don't know.

SHAYLEE: Why not?

WYNNE: *(Mumbling.)* Cause I've never seen her.

SHAYLEE: What?

WYNNE: I've never seen her. I met her online. And so what if she was?

SHAYLEE: Niggers are dirty. Trust me, I know. Where's she from?

WYNNE: Crothersville, Indiana.

SHAYLEE: Small-town nigger, to boot.

WYNNE: If Ma heard you say nigger she'd fuckin' die.

SHAYLEE: So.

WYNNE: So, you sound like one of those skinheads from Cicero.

SHAYLEE: I like those guys.

WYNNE: You're a racist.

SHAYLEE: No I ain't. I just don't like niggers.

(He gives her the finger. She descends the stairs, crosses to him on the sofa.)

SHAYLEE: Do you jerk off to her?

WYNNE: To who?

SHAYLEE: Shaniqua.

WYNNE: Sharice.

SHAYLEE: Sharice. You beat your meat to Sharice?

WYNNE: Sometimes.

(She administers a titanic titty twister.)

SHAYLEE: Cum on your stomach, think about tastin' it?

WYNNE: *(Wrenching away.)* Fuck no! . . . What time is it, anyway?

SHAYLEE: Time to fuck and buy drugs. Why?

WYNNE: She's s'posed to call.

SHAYLEE: Phone sex.

WYNNE: I'm in love with her, Shaylee.

SHAYLEE: Nigger phone sex.

WYNNE: We instant-message each other all the time. We're goin to New York together. I'm hitchin' to Crothersville and then we're taking Greyhound the rest of the way.

SHAYLEE: Where the fuck is Crothersville?

WYNNE: Somewhere in the middle of the state, offa 65. She's mute.

SHAYLEE: How the fuck is she gonna call here if she's mute?

WYNNE: She's got this thing that she types into. Some sorta transmitter. An electronic voice speaks into the phone based on what she types.

SHAYLEE: *(Getting off the sofa.)* That's so fucked.

WYNNE: I think it's cool.

(Shaylee crosses to the kitchen.)

SHAYLEE: What if the voice is all macho or somethin'?

WYNNE: I don't care.

SHAYLEE: What if she sounds like a cop?

WYNNE: I really don't care. I think I'm in love.

SHAYLEE: *(From the kitchen.)* You better fuck her before you start talkin' about love, Wynne.

WYNNE: Why?

SHAYLEE: *(Re-entering with a bottle of liquor.)* Cause her pussy might be dry. *(Shaylee crosses to the sofa, sits. Wynne follows her.)*

WYNNE: I ain't in love with her pussy.

SHAYLEE: What are you in love with, her e-mail address?

WYNNE: I don't know, Shaylee. I don't have the slightest idea what she looks like and I'm totally in love with her. And tell me this isn't weird: You know how my e-mail address is dog on mars at mindspring dot com? Well, hers is dog on venus at mindspring dot com. Pretty fuckin' trippy, huh?

SHAYLEE: Romeo and Juliet.

WYNNE: *(Sitting on the sofa.)* Mars and Venus, man.

SHAYLEE: Romeoville and Joliet.

(Shaylee takes a slug of vodka, almost retches.)

SHAYLEE: So you're still playin' that video game, huh?

WYNNE: Yeah, I solved it. That's why I'm a finalist.

SHAYLEE: Fuckin' genius.

WYNNE: There's only three of us. They're gonna film the championship. Put it on cable.

SHAYLEE: Wynne the boy genius.

WYNNE: I ain't a boy.

SHAYLEE: If I cracked your head open I bet your brain would be huge.

WYNNE: If I win I'm gonna send you some money, Shaylee. You can go to that place in Michigan with the maple trees.

SHAYLEE: Fuck the maple trees.

WYNNE: You're gonna die if you don't get help.

SHAYLEE: I met this guy at a truck stop. His name was Jesus. He looked like Art Garfunkel if Art Garfunkel was a spic. He told me my soul was floatin' around somewhere in the stratosphere. He kept callin' me a floater. I fucked him in Centralia while I was on my period and I had to go to this clinic cause I forgot to take my tampon out.

This doctor had to remove it with salad tongs. Fuckin' place was full of refugees and derelicts.

WYNNE: You can take whatever you want outta my room.

SHAYLEE: What would I take?

WYNNE: Take my Playstation 2. You could prolly get fifty bucks for it.

SHAYLEE: You don't want your fuckin' Playstation?

WYNNE: It's too easy.

(She smokes.)

SHAYLEE: This chick I met at the Y told me you can kill yourself by slashin' your wrists in the bathtub. She said it don't hurt if you make the water warm enough cause it tricks your brain. . . .

(They both sit up.)

WYNNE: You better go.

SHAYLEE: You ain't gonna give me five bucks?

(He goes in his pocket, produces two. She snatches the cash.)

SHAYLEE: I'll suck your dick for two more. . . .

WYNNE: You really gonna buy a gun?

SHAYLEE: *(Mocking.)* You really gonna buy a gun? . . .

(Shaylee kisses him hard on the mouth, exits quickly up the stairs. Wynne exits.)

VALHALLA
Paul Rudnick

Seriocomic
Sally, seventeen; James, a little older

> *Sally is getting married to her high school sweetheart. James is a*
> *bad boy just out of reform school. He wants Sally for himself; or,*
> *rather, he wants to deprive his buddy of his bride. Lights up on Sally,*
> *wearing a pretty, frilly bathrobe, seated before her vanity table, fac-*
> *ing the audience. A deluxe, full-length wedding gown is worn by*
> *a dressmaking mannequin that stands nearby. She might brush her*
> *hair and apply makeup. It's her wedding day, and she's on a sin-*
> *cere spiritual quest.*

JAMES: The front door was open.

SALLY: Is that really you? Are you back?

JAMES: For the day.

SALLY: Look at you, you look, well, I'm not even sure what to say, you look — older. Rougher. But what are you doing here?

JAMES: *(Moving toward the wedding gown.)* It's this afternoon, isn't it?

SALLY: Why yes, yes it is.

> *(As James is about to touch the gown.)*

French silk — please don't touch that.

JAMES: You sent me all of those sweet letters, at least once a month, with all of those charming tidbits, about the town and the school . . .

SALLY: Did I tell you about my mother's new car?

JAMES: The Buick.

SALLY: And my dad's business?

JAMES: Just booming.

SALLY: Although I am so worried about things in Europe . . .

JAMES: I remember — "P.S., It's sad about Poland."

SALLY: Isn't it?

JAMES: But somehow you never mentioned Henry Lee.

SALLY: Well, he wasn't invaded, now was he?

JAMES: Oh really?

SALLY: Now James, I'm sorry, and it's not that it isn't a wonderful surprise to see you, but my parents are at the church, making sure that everything is just perfect, and my Maid of Honor will be here any minute. Do you remember Emmeline Atwood?

JAMES: The blind girl?

SALLY: But I told her — no dog.

JAMES: So we're alone.

SALLY: James?

JAMES: How could you? With Henry Lee?

SALLY: How could I resist? I mean, he is so handsome, and I don't want to brag, but you should have seen us, we were King and Queen at the Prom. Oh I'm sorry, where you were, did they even have a Prom?

JAMES: Of course. And we each picked a younger, smaller boy and pretended he was our date.

SALLY: That is so sweet. Was there a theme?

JAMES: "Just Relax."

SALLY: Now James, I know that I was naughty, not to tell you about our plans. And I'm sorry that I can't invite you to the wedding, but it's a Christian ceremony, and you're, well . . .

JAMES: Satan?

SALLY: *(Sincerely.)* Thank you.

JAMES: Do you love him?

SALLY: He's the president of our class . . .

JAMES: Do you love him?

SALLY: My parents worship the ground he walks on . . .

JAMES: Do you love him?

SALLY: Stop asking that!

JAMES: Look at me.

SALLY: I don't want to. You look crude, and unshaven, and — unreformed.

JAMES: Ever since we were little, I've known all about you. You are so good and so pretty and so perfect . . .

SALLY: Because I make an effort. And I stay out of the sun.

JAMES: And today you're getting married, to the perfect boy.

SALLY: Yes I am.

JAMES: Because you have so much in common.

SALLY: That's right.

JAMES: Because in just a few short hours, on your wedding night, you will both be thinking about *me*.

SALLY: You are disgusting! You are just what everyone says you are!

JAMES: A thief?

SALLY: Can you deny it?

JAMES: And a pansy?

SALLY: Well, isn't it true? Isn't that why you want Henry Lee?

JAMES: Not right now.

SALLY: James?

JAMES: I want everything. Everything beautiful.

SALLY: James?

JAMES: I want you.

SALLY: I am getting married! This afternoon!

JAMES: So there's still time.

SALLY: You went away. You left me here. So I started to hate you. So I decided to steal something. Something you wanted.

JAMES: What if I came over there, right now, and kissed you? What would you do? Would you slap my face?

SALLY: Yes I would.

(James goes to her and kisses her. She slaps him.)

JAMES: What if I kissed you again? Would you call the police?

SALLY: Watch me.

(James kisses her again.)

SALLY: *(In a tiny voice.)* Police . . .

JAMES: And what if I picked you up and carried you to that bed? What if I made love to you? Would you yell "Stop, oh please, stop"?

SALLY: Yes.

JAMES: Then good-bye. I won't make you do anything you don't want to do.

(James starts to leave.)

SALLY: James?

JAMES: Yeah?

SALLY: Stop.

(Sally drops her robe and stands in just her slip. James picks her up, and carries her offstage.)

WAKE GOD'S MAN
Julie Marie Myatt

Dramatic
Beth and Man, could be any age

> *The characters appear to be dead, in some kind of limbo. He was a priest. The body bag is empty and the body is gone from above the stage. The Man enters with a broom and sweeps the pecan shells across the stage.*

MAN: There's always a trace of something left behind from the appetites of man. Always a crack or a shell or a wrapper or a sock or a feather or a trail of blood. A laugh. A scream. A voice . . . Unheard. Somewhere. Left behind. Somewhere in the wake. Of the action . . . *(Continues to sweep.)* . . . what a mess, these nuts — so much trouble just to get that little bite of pleasure — I call them *pecans,* while some call them *peecans* — I guess I can't help myself. I must have a few guilty pleasures. You think you can give them all up, and you do, you do, give them up, but the appetite — the appetite has a mind of its own, and I'm not sure I was expecting that — I was a young man when I was called, Idealist, what did I know? — and I'm not sure God understands how powerful that appetite is, that to give it up is — is not always possible.
> *(Beth enters. Kicks a pecan shell toward him.)*
BETH: You missed one.
MAN: Thanks.
BETH: Who you talking to?
MAN: No one.
BETH: God abandon you?
MAN: Perhaps.
BETH: Good.
> *(He continues to sweep.)*

MAN: You always did have a sharp tongue . . . Of course, I always liked
your family. Good sense of humor. I enjoyed your company.

BETH: I am aware of that tragedy. Your hatred would have been more welcome. Sir.

MAN: Well, your hatred is not welcome here, at the moment, if that's what
you've come for. I'm tired. Confused. And dead.

BETH: No kidding.

(She looks him over.)

So this is what you looked like as a young man?

MAN: This is the way I remember. Myself.

BETH: Dig the hair. Very stylish.

MAN: I thought so.

BETH: Hell. At least you had hair then. I still want to vomit every time I
think of the top of your bald head. The way the sweat would bead
up on that oily skin. Bastard —

MAN: Move along. I don't like that kind of talk. I've got work to do.

BETH: Oh?

MAN: There's mess everywhere.

BETH: God making you earn your keep now? Or is that the devil's work?
Or. Could be Limbo. I've heard that's a pretty irritating place to be.

(He looks at her.)

MAN: Depends on the company . . . You know, I worked hard every day
of my life —

BETH: At hiding things —

MAN: Serving people —

BETH: Silencing —

MAN: Bringing God into open hearts —

BETH: Putting fear into sacred places —

MAN: Providing refuge —

BETH: Stealing childhoods.

MAN: And this is the thanks I get.

BETH: You want wings?

MAN: Do you want revenge?

BETH: I want my childhood back.

MAN: Who doesn't? *(Beth hadn't considered that. Silence. Man keeps sweep-
ing.)* We all suffer something. I had my faults, but what I gave to so

many cannot be compared to what I might have — what you think I've taken from you . . . I was the eyes and ears and conscience of this town, without judgment —

BETH: How could you judge, when your sins were worse, were greater, so much more serious than any you might have heard?

MAN: I was a good man.

BETH: No. You were not.

MAN: I was a good man with, with, appetites that I tried to control, I tried very hard, but even I could not control some things — I gave up everything for this church. For this occupation. I gave up everything that I watched my congregation enjoy.

BETH: You picked the job. No one put a gun to your head and made you be a priest —

MAN: He made me. He picked me. I was Called. Do you know how much pressure, how much sacrifice, how much responsibility that is?

BETH: That sacrifice, that responsibility was just too much? Keeping your hands off young girls was just too much to ask, too much pressure? —

MAN: I once tried to kill myself. Does that make you feel better?

BETH: No.

MAN: But I was afraid of what would happen. After.

BETH: Fire and brimstone?

MAN: Worse. This. Cold reunion. The infinity of disgust. *(He looks directly at her.)* I am, I was a good man. So very many prayers brushed across my lips in one lifetime — kisses to the heavens — but, those, those . . . I don't know what to call them — did not, could not, come close enough for discussion. It was lonely. To tell Him all my secrets but the frightened ones that ask, that might have asked, for the biggest kind of forgiveness — You don't understand. I tried to control myself. I'm sorry but I did try. I tried —

(Beth rips the broom from his hands.)

BETH: No. Sir. You didn't. Try.

(She brushes the pile of shells across the floor.)

MAN: I did *try.* Every day —

BETH: *Try?* . . . *Try* and tell that "poor me" story to someone who gives a shit. You will not get my forgiveness or peace or compassion. You made your bed. You made those choices, you did those things, that ruined my sisters. And me. You *did* those things, *to* us. You earned that disgust. You get nothing from me but contempt and good-bye. *(Beth gives him back the broom. She walks offstage.)*

Scenes for
Two Men

BIRDY
Naomi Wallace

Dramatic
Young Al and Young Birdy, teens

> *Al and Birdy are best buddies. Al calls his friend "Birdy" because of his fascination with birds.*

> *Young Al and Young Birdy in Birdy's bedroom. Young Birdy stands uncomfortably in a rented tux.*

YOUNG BIRDY: I feel like a freak.

YOUNG AL: If you'd stop sweating you'd be fine.

YOUNG BIRDY: I can't do it, Al. Call Doris. Tell her I broke my leg.

YOUNG AL: You look great.

YOUNG BIRDY: *(Starts to take off his tux.)* I never wanted to go. You wanted me to go. My mother wanted me to go.

YOUNG AL: You're just nervous. No. You're fucking scared.

YOUNG BIRDY: Yeah. I am.

YOUNG AL: It'll be a breeze.

YOUNG BIRDY: I can't talk to girls.

YOUNG AL: Doris is practically a woman.

YOUNG BIRDY: That's even worse. Al. I can't do it. I just can't do it. Please.

YOUNG AL: OK. Get up. Get up. I'm Doris.

YOUNG BIRDY: What?

YOUNG AL: I'm Doris and you're you and you're at first base.

YOUNG BIRDY: First base.

YOUNG AL: Right. Sitting together in the car. Her car. After the dance. It's dark outside. You're parked by the lake.
(Young Al sits down. He motions for Young Birdy to sit beside him.)
Now. Doris is still wearing the orchid and she asks you to unpin it.

YOUNG BIRDY: I hate orchids. No way I'm touching one.

YOUNG AL: Damn it, Birdy. Unpin the orchid.

YOUNG BIRDY: Where is it?

YOUNG AL: Just over the breast. And its a big one. A big fucking orchid.

YOUNG BIRDY: As big as a pigeon.

YOUNG AL: Right. And it's still fresh cause she kept it in the fridge all day.

YOUNG BIRDY: That's as good a place as any for something that smells dead.

YOUNG AL: *(Speaks as Doris but uses his own voice. He does not "play" a woman, either in voice or physical movements.)* Could you take off my orchid, Birdy?

YOUNG BIRDY: I guess so. *(He fumbles at the imaginary orchid on Young Al's shirt and unpins it.)* Ow. It pricked me.

YOUNG AL: I'm sorry, Birdy. Is it bleeding?

YOUNG BIRDY: Just a bit.

YOUNG AL: Let me see.

> *("Doris" examines Young Birdy's finger, then sucks on it. After a moment, Young Birdy pulls his hand back. They tug back and forth.)*

YOUNG AL: Give me your fucking finger, Birdy. Doris is bound to make the first move and you have to go for it. You've pricked your finger and now she's going to suck on it. Bat 'er up.

YOUNG BIRDY: Bat 'er up?

YOUNG AL: Make your move. Go for it. She sucks your finger and you let her. Then she turns to you. Her face is soft.

YOUNG BIRDY: As a baby bird.

YOUNG AL: Her cape is pulled back and she looks almost naked. She reaches over and turns on the radio. It's Glenn Miller's "Sunrise Serenade."

YOUNG BIRDY: I like that song.

YOUNG AL: You love it.

YOUNG BIRDY: It has the inside completeness of a good canary song.

YOUNG AL: So Doris turns to you and suddenly you know you're a candle on her cake and you're just about to be blown out. Anything can happen.

YOUNG BIRDY: Anything can happen and I know it's going to be embarrassing.

YOUNG AL: Doris climbs up onto her knees. In the darkness you see she's left her shoes down there by the accelerator. Doris is humming to the music and you put your arm around her. Go on.

> *(Young Birdy does so.)*

YOUNG AL: And now it's up to you.

YOUNG BIRDY: *(After some moments.)* You like this song? *(Beat.)* Doris.

YOUNG AL: Go.

YOUNG BIRDY: Go?

YOUNG AL: Do it. Kiss her. It's what she's been waiting for.

(Young Birdy gives Young Al a hesitant kiss on the cheek.)

YOUNG AL: Now to second base.

YOUNG BIRDY: I have no idea, Al.

YOUNG AL: Jesus, Birdy. You're never gonna make it as a man in this world. Now shut up and unbutton her dress.

YOUNG BIRDY: I can't do that. That's disgusting.

YOUNG AL: Unbutton her dress. When you see her tits you won't be thinking disgusting.

(Young Birdy fumbles with the buttons on Young Al's shirt.)

YOUNG BIRDY: I won't be thinking disgusting. I won't be thinking disgusting.

YOUNG AL: Take your time. There's no rush. Doris is breathing into your mouth and sucking in.

(Young Birdy now takes his time to open Young Al's shirt.)

YOUNG BIRDY: I feel the air being pulled in through my nostrils.

YOUNG AL: Holy God! This is kissing and Doris is some kind of a vampire stealing your breath. And, you can't believe it, you're getting a hard-on!

YOUNG BIRDY: *(Looking down at his crotch.)* I am? Yes I am. And I try to cross my legs, to hide it, maybe to crank it down.

YOUNG AL: But there's no fooling Doris. She's shoving her stomach right into it! She moans.

YOUNG BIRDY: And pushes her tongue in deeper.

(Young Birdy has undone all of Young Al's buttons.)

YOUNG AL: And then her tits pop out.

YOUNG BIRDY: And they look better than the ones in the *National Geographic.*

(Young Birdy suddenly opens Young Al's shirt and puts both his hands on Young Al's breasts. He squeezes and touches them.)

YOUNG AL: Yeah. Well. I suppose you should just grab em. That's right. Just dive in.

YOUNG BIRDY: You work out too much, Al.

YOUNG AL: These are pecs. Not breasts. Pecs.

(Young Birdy drops his hand.)

YOUNG BIRDY: *(Goes to his birdcages again.)* I don't want to fuck, Doris. You want me to fuck Doris. Who knows what my mother wants. *(Beat.)* But I'm going. OK? I'll pin on the orchid. I'll dance with her. I'll even slow dance. But that's all I'll promise you.

CHECK, PLEASE
Jonathan Rand

Comic
Melanie and Guy, twenties

> *Melanie and Guy are a couple on a date. This scene will work best*
> *if Melanie is truly sweet, innocent, and adorable when she's focused*
> *on the date.*

GUY: Hi.

MELANIE: Hi.

GUY: It's so great to finally meet you.

MELANIE: Same here!

GUY: So . . . What do you —

MELANIE: Wait, before you — Sorry. *(Meekly.)* This is so rude, but the Bears games is on right now? You don't mind if I check the score . . .

GUY: Oh sure. Totally.

MELANIE: *(As she pulls out her cell phone to check her Web-browser.)* Thanks. I know this is such an awful thing to do on a first date, but it's late in the fourth quarter, and it's do-or-die if we wanna make the playoffs.

GUY: It's no problem at all. Really.

MELANIE: Thanks. *(As she checks.)* I love the Bears. They're really strong this season — well-rounded. *(Sees score; reacts a little.)* OK, I'm done. *(Cheerily:)* That wasn't so bad, was it?

GUY: What's the score?

MELANIE: Packers by seven.

GUY: Uh-oh.

MELANIE: Nah, it's no big deal. It's just a game, right? So c'mon — enough about football. Let's hear about "Mister Mystery." Harriet's told me tons about you.

GUY: Man . . . The pressure's on now.

(They laugh together, genuinely. Melanie's laugh then fades directly into her next line, which is suddenly serious.)

MELANIE: I'm just gonna check on the game one more time.

(She digs into her purse.)

GUY: *(Smiling.)* No worries.

MELANIE: Is it all right with you if I put on this little earpiece thingy? It won't be distracting, I promise.

GUY: Sure.

MELANIE: *(As she puts the earpiece in her ear:)* I'm making the worst first impression, aren't I?

GUY: Not at all.

MELANIE: It's just because it's for the play-offs. I'm usually pretty normal.

GUY: It's really no —

MELANIE: *(Throws her hands up:)* Ah!

GUY: What?

MELANIE: Oh. Nothing. The line only gave A-Train this enormous running lane, but he fumbles after two yards. The ball rolled out of bounds, so we're cool, but come on — it's for the playoffs. You don't just drop the ball like that, you know? Now you're third and long, and the whole season is riding on one play.

GUY: That's —

MELANIE: WHAT?!

GUY: What?

MELANIE: PASS THE BALL!

GUY: What's wrong?

MELANIE: Miller! He doesn't pass it. The man refuses to pass the ball this season. It's third and long — Who hands it off on third and long? Is he suddenly AFRAID OF HIS RECEIVERS?!

(Guy looks around subtly at the other patrons.)

Oh my God, I'm sorry. I'm being loud, aren't I.

GUY: *(Trying hard to be convincing:)* No . . .

MELANIE: Oh, I am. I'm so sorry. Look, how about this: *(She tenderly takes his hands in hers.)* I'll make it up to you. After dinner I'll buy you dessert at this tiny little bistro on 11th that nobody knows about. It's gotta be one of my absolute favorite places to go. It's so precious. I think you'll just

PASS THE BALL!! Jesus, people! This is FOOTBALL, not FREEZE TAG. It's FOURTH DOWN — pass the FRIGGING BALL!

GUY: Listen — we could go to a bar or something if you want — watch the game on TV.

MELANIE: Oh please no, I wouldn't do that to you. The game's basically over. *(She takes a deep breath, and is now very calm.)* OK. I'm done. I got a little carried away there, didn't I? Let's order.

(They peruse for a moment, as if nothing has happened.)

GUY: Oh. *(Indicating the menu:)* Harriet said we should definitely try the — *(Melanie suddenly lets out a bloodcurdling shriek and rips the menu in half. Beat.)*

GUY: Or, we could order something else. *(Beat.)* Your menu tore a little.

MELANIE: *(Downtrodden.)* They lost . . .

GUY: Oh. Oh, I'm sorry.

MELANIE: *(Starting to tear up.)* They lost. They just blew the play-offs.

GUY: Well, I —

(Melanie breaks down, bawling. Guy thinks for a moment, then takes out a handkerchief and offers it to Melanie. She uses it to blow her nose.)

GUY: I'm so sorry. Can I do anything to help?

MELANIE: *(Still weepy:)* The Bears suck . . .

GUY: Aww, no. They don't suck.

MELANIE: They do . . . They suck.

GUY: They're probably just having a bad season —

(Melanie grabs his collar, pulls him extremely close, and speaks in a horrifying, monstrous voice.)

MELANIE: THE BEARS SUCK.

GUY: *(Very weakly.)* The Bears suck.

(Blackout.)

THE DAZZLE
Richard Greenberg

Seriocomic
Homer and Lang, thirties

> The Dazzle *is a dazzling dark comedy inspired by the strange story of the Collyer brothers. Homer and Lang are two very eccentric brothers who live together in an old NYC mansion. Homer, the more functional of the two, works as a lawyer. Lang used to be a concert pianist, but he has no bookings anymore because his tempo has slowed to a snail's pace. As this scene begins, Lang has just finished playing "The Minute Waltz" — in about forty-five minutes. Homer has had enough. Desperate steps must be taken.*

LANG: Were you speaking to me before?

HOMER: Yes.

LANG: I wasn't listening. *(Beat.)*

HOMER: Ah.

LANG: I was playing.

HOMER: Yes. I heard. It was very impressive. You completed "The Minute Waltz" in slightly under three-quarters of an hour —

LANG: It was quite nice —

HOMER: Next year this time, you'll have to take an intermission.

LANG: Are you *upset?*

HOMER: . . . Of course not.

LANG: You are, though. I think you are. Why? Be specific.

HOMER: No reason. No reason at all.

LANG: It doesn't have anything to do with *me,* does it?

HOMER: How could it? *(Pause.)* You need to get things under control, Lang.

LANG: What things?

HOMER: You need — are you listening to me now?

LANG: Yes —

HOMER: Are you really?

LANG: I'm not playing —

HOMER: All right. You need to — conduct yourself in a more — well, *don't* listen like *that* — please —

LANG: Like what?

HOMER: With such — rapt — concentration —

LANG: Why not?

HOMER: Because, in the first place, I'm not going to say anything delightful. In the second place, there are — there *should* be — natural modulations to — the art of listening — and, in the third place — it's just creepy.

LANG: I'm sorry, Homer.

HOMER: That's — fine — look — you have to conduct your business in a more businesslike way.

LANG: Ah. *(Beat.)* I don't know what that means.

HOMER: It means — for example — you have to stick to your word.

LANG: I do stick to my word, Homer —

HOMER: Lang —

LANG: Or — well — actually — it's more like my *words* stick to *me* — I mean — I speak in a kind of stream — and usually — I try to do whatever it was I said last.

HOMER: That's not how business is conducted.

LANG: It *ought* to be.

HOMER: But it *can't*. If in September of 1904 you promise to perform Schubert at such-and-such a place in August of 1905, you are expected to perform Schubert at such-and-such a place in August of 1905.

LANG: Well, that's ridiculous.

HOMER: It isn't.

LANG: It *is* and I'm not going to explain why because I just don't have the wind for it, at the moment. You should know, anyway, Homer; you should know why. *(Beat. Homer sits.)*

HOMER: Do you want to be old and sick and hungry and without a home?

LANG: I can't say. I haven't tried.

HOMER: *Would you please care enough about me to* accept *a premise?*

LANG: . . . Yes, Homer, I'm sorry.

HOMER: We are not in trouble at the moment —

LANG: Then may I go?

HOMER: But we *may be* shortly.

LANG: . . . Hm. Ah. How shortly?

HOMER: I don't — does it matter?

LANG: Yes.

HOMER: . . . *Very* shortly.

LANG: "Very." Timid, empty stark little word.

HOMER: Tomorrow, the day after, ten years from now — all I am saying is we have to take *the long view* — *(Lang returns to piano, plays a chord, holds it.) Lang!*

LANG: Do you hear that —

HOMER: All Harlem hears that —

LANG: . . . If that were true . . .

HOMER: I am so sick of these chords you bang out — at random — night and day — they reverberate endlessly — they've worked their way into the curtains, I swear it, like some old bad stench of cigar smoke or —

LANG: Most smells are actually pleasant if you don't know where they're coming from.

HOMER: *(Slams hands onto piano top.)* Lang!

LANG: . . . Yes, Homer?

HOMER: What do you think of the girl?

LANG: What girl?

HOMER: Oh Lord — the girl — the girl — the rich girl — who sits beside me at your recitals — and swoons and gasps and sways as though she were the music — what do you think of her?

LANG: Mildred.

HOMER: Yes.

LANG: Milly.

HOMER: Yes.

LANG: Her name is Milly.

HOMER: That does not constitute an opinion.

LANG: Doesn't it?

HOMER: I believe that she's in love with you. *(Pause.)*

LANG: Huh. Is that . . . ? Really.

HOMER: I believe so.

LANG: What does that mean? Tell me exactly. Turn on the lamps first.

HOMER: It isn't dark.

LANG: It will be when you finish.

HOMER: I am not going to go . . . into all that.

LANG: Why not?

HOMER: Because . . . it isn't definable.

LANG: Then on what authority do you speak of it?

HOMER: One can . . . *feel* it, without . . . being able to . . . put into words —

LANG: I don't agree — I think a word can exist without a meaning but a meaning can't exist without a word — music is better than either, because it forgoes both — that's why I hate books — books always seem to me like music explaining itself under duress. But what were you saying?

HOMER: I don't remember.

LANG: Love! That was it. You were going to define it.

HOMER: I was attempting *not* to —

LANG: Because you've never experienced it? *(Beat.)*

HOMER: You live only to torture me, don't you?

LANG: Not at all.

HOMER: I *have* — experienced —

LANG: Oh poo — *where? When?*

HOMER: Lang —

LANG: When you were away?

HOMER: Yes.

LANG: When you were away in — oh, what is China always called in the disintegrating books — *Cathay?*

HOMER: Among other places.

LANG: Really?

HOMER: Yes.

LANG: Really?

HOMER: Yes!

LANG: Oh, Homer, why must you lie *at home?* Lying is for outdoors — this is our house!

HOMER: I am *not* — I have a very real past —

LANG: There is no such thing —

HOMER: I . . . have . . . had . . . have had . . . one. For all the good it does me now. I was . . . a different person. Before. You must grant me that, it's my solace. Oh Christ Christ Christ Christ, why are we — *(Pause. He sits.)* I know you can't answer this next question, but I'll ask it anyway: Do you love her?

LANG: Oh, I can answer that.

HOMER: You can?

LANG: Yes. I know what love is; you're the one who can't define it. Do I love her? Yes. I believe I do.

HOMER: Truly?

LANG: Yes. I believe so. There's something . . . miasmic about her.

HOMER: Miasmic?

LANG: Yes. It's her speech! It's when she speaks. You see, she has nothing to say; and she says it incessantly. There's never a phrase, a word — an accent, even — that hasn't been thoroughly modified by convention, made virtually inaudible by overuse. She's so ordinary! It's as though ordinariness had been rubbed into the very *nap* of her voice — her voice lulls me! — It has none of the hooks and snares of most voices — why, Homer, she very nearly bores me, and hardly anything does that! I can imagine living with her as one would beside a narrow and uninteresting body of water — scarcely even aware of its existence — yet made utterly tranquil by its flow. Yes. I love her. And sex is not a problem for me, you know. I mean, it's no more intense than anything else. *(Pause.)*

HOMER: Well, then . . .

LANG: Why do you ask?

HOMER: No reason. *(Beat.)* She's very rich. *(Beat.)* No reason.

DEPARTURES
John Godber

Dramatic
Jim and Steve, thirties to forties

> *Jim and Steve are two business executives. They do a lot of travel-*
> *ing together, spending a lot of time in airports. Whereas Steve is*
> *morally loose, maintaining a string of relationships with women, Jim*
> *is determined to be exactly the opposite — faithful and true to his*
> *wife. Easier said than done. Steve and Jim recline and stretch.*

STEVE: All right, then?

JIM: Not bad.

STEVE: How's Annie?

JIM: Great . . .

STEVE: How's the boyfriend?

JIM: Older than me!

STEVE: A lot in common, then?

JIM: Oh, don't!

    (A beat.)

STEVE: Had a good time, then?

JIM: Ay, not bad.

STEVE: Good.

    (A beat.)

JIM: Is everything all right?

STEVE: Yes.

JIM: I thought I could just detect . . .

STEVE: What?

JIM: I don't know, I just thought . . .

STEVE: No, man, everything's fine! *(He is looking at Steve.)*

JIM: Is it?

STEVE: Course it is!

    (A beat.)

JIM: *(Starting to cry.)* That's all right, then?

STEVE: Hey, man?

JIM: Sorry, mate.

STEVE: Hey . . .

JIM: Oh dear . . .

STEVE: You OK?

JIM: Jet lag, man!

STEVE: Oh hell!

(A beat.)

JIM: Just seeing her again . . .

STEVE: Oh man!

JIM: Oh hell . . .

STEVE: Hey, come on . . .

JIM: This is serious . . .

STEVE: I can see that . . .

(A beat.)

JIM: I'm leaving Claire . . .

STEVE: What?

JIM: I'm leaving her . . .

STEVE: Oh, man . . .

JIM: I've told her, I'm moving out!

STEVE: Oh, man!

JIM: Getting a flat!

STEVE: Oh!

JIM: Jeeez . . .

(A beat.)

STEVE: Man, are you sure?

JIM: Oh ay . . . We erm . . . I don't know, I can't go on with her!

STEVE: Oh dear.

JIM: And now I've met Zoë I know it's right!

STEVE: Oh, right.

JIM: I thought it might go away but . . .

STEVE: Right, then!

JIM: I never felt like this about Claire. Even when I first met her.

STEVE: Man, you've got twenty odd years . . .

JIM: I know.

STEVE: That's a religion.

JIM: I love her.

STEVE: Yes.

JIM: It's as simple as that . . .

STEVE: Man, do you know her?

JIM: It's real, mate! Just looking at her and I'm all over the shop . . .
    (A beat.)

STEVE: Man . . .

JIM: I am . . .

STEVE: Oh!

JIM: It's the only way I can explain it!
    (A beat.)

STEVE: Man, I think there's been a . . .
    (A beat.)

JIM: Wha . . .

STEVE: Man . . .

JIM: What?

STEVE: Oh hell . . .
    (A beat.)

JIM: Oh, man!

STEVE: Sorry.

JIM: Eh?

STEVE: I'm not a King . . . !

JIM: Oh . . . !

STEVE: Like you said, dangerous!

JIM: Oh . . . !

STEVE: I didn't think it was so . . .

JIM: I told you . . .

STEVE: I know, but . . .

JIM: I told you as a mate . . .

STEVE: I know you did, but . . .

JIM: Fuckin' hell, Steve!

STEVE: I know, I know!

JIM: What did you think I was telling you for, a laugh?

STEVE: Well, I thought I was doing you a favor.

JIM: Oh, that's the best thing I've ever heard!

STEVE: Look, listen, I partly did if for you.

JIM: Oh, thanks!

STEVE: I did it for Claire.

JIM: That's right!

STEVE: I did it for the company.

JIM: You did it for your fucking self.

STEVE: It just happened!

JIM: I even asked you not to . . .

STEVE: You're torturing yourself . . .

JIM: Oh man!

STEVE: Anyway, you had your chance!

JIM: It's not about that, it's about friendship.

STEVE: Oh!

JIM: It is.

STEVE: Oh!

JIM: It is.

STEVE: So what's changed?

JIM: Oh dear . . .

STEVE: She's still your mate.

JIM: I'm pathetic . . .

STEVE: Mate, you can say it's none of my business but don't throw away all you've got . . .

JIM: It's too late for that, Stevie boy . . .

STEVE: Listen, if there's ever a trouser factor you can't be a mate with 'em.

JIM: So you can only be a mate with ugly women?

STEVE: Well, I can!

JIM: This is why you wanted her to work for us!

STEVE: Oh, come on . . .

JIM: Give up. I know you . . . That's why you tried it on in Spain, and it means nothing to you.

STEVE: Well, I wouldn't go that far.

JIM: I would.

(A beat.)

STEVE: You don't want to leave Claire . . . you're made for each other . . .

JIM: So what happened, then, did she just come out with it?

STEVE: No, we stayed in Manchester because of the weather.

JIM: Oh, right.

STEVE: She . . . . erm . . . knew this Czech woman or sommat.

JIM: Oh, right.

STEVE: Went to her flat. The three of us. I'm not a King, man.

JIM: Oh, Jesus!

STEVE: I'm not a King.

JIM: Got a bit further than the kissing this time, then?

STEVE: Who with?

JIM: Bloody hell! *(He begins to cry. He cries hard and then the crying turns into a cackle of laughter. He moves downstage.)* Oh, hell, eh? Flying, wonderful, why do I put myself through this!

STEVE: I only had one night, man . . .

JIM: That's right . . .

STEVE: One night . . .

JIM: Yes!

STEVE: You've had twenty odd years.

JIM: That's right.

STEVE: Not worth it.

JIM: That's right.

STEVE: You're lucky, mate.

JIM: I am, aren't I?

STEVE: You're a King!

JIM: King Jim of Shipley!

    (Steve stands.)

STEVE: I'm going to get a drink, do you want one?

JIM: No, thanks . . .

DIRTY STORY
John Patrick Shanley

Comic

Frank, twenties to thirties; the bartender Watson, any age

> *Frank, a cowboy, is hanging out in a bar talking to the bartender.*
> *Music. The cowboy, Frank, sits at a bar tossing cards into his hat.*
> *He's gained a lot of weight. Watson, the bartender, a Cockney, looks*
> *on. It's the same guy who played Lawrence; he raises a sign that says:*
> *NONFICTION. The music fades, replaced by Frank singing. Wat-*
> *son sweeps up.*

FRANK: *Camp Town races sing this song*

WATSON: *Do dah! Do dah!*

FRANK: *Camp Town race is way too long*

WATSON: *Oh da do dah day!*

FRANK: *Goin' to run all night*

WATSON: Right.

FRANK: *Goin' to run all day*

WATSON: True.

FRANK: *Bet my money on a bobtailed nag*

WATSON: Ouch.

FRANK: *Somebody bet on the gray*

WATSON: Tragic, isn't it?

FRANK: No customers. Not a single Goddamn customer. What happened
   to the drinking public?

WATSON: Take it easy. Why would there be any customers, Frank? It's Sunday morning and we're closed.

FRANK: Maybe we should open?

WATSON: The law says no serving of alcoholic beverages on Sunday morning. It's to promote churchgoing I believe.

FRANK: Church. You go?

WATSON: Not for years. You?

FRANK: Sometimes, but I have trouble with it.

WATSON: Doubt?

FRANK: No, envy. I don't wanna worship, I wanna preach.

WATSON: It's my impression that religions were organized AGAINST God. Like labor unions.

FRANK: Labor unions! Are you trying to get my goat?

WATSON: Not a bit.

FRANK: Are you trying to get health benefits?

WATSON: No, no! I have a perfectly nice little first-aid kit! *(Watson has fled behind the bar. Frank starts as if he heard something. Impasse.)*

FRANK: Can't you feel it?

WATSON: What?

FRANK: The silence.

WATSON: Maybe you should *(Knocks.)* let it in?

FRANK: I don't think so, kimosabe. I prefer noise and toys. *(Frank pulls out a pack of cigarettes and slams them on the bar.)* Try this on.

WATSON: What's this?

FRANK: Pack a cigarettes.

WATSON: What good's that do me? I don't smoke.

FRANK: Maybe you could start.

WATSON: Why?

FRANK: Try one on the house.

WATSON: Why would I do that?

FRANK: You might like it.

WATSON: Bloody Hell, so much the worse. I get addicted. Do you smoke?

FRANK: I quit. That shit'll kill ya.

WATSON: I don't want the cigarettes. *(Frank snatches the pack back.)*

FRANK: All right, so don't have one.

WATSON: Well, you don't have to be like that about it.

FRANK: Oh, I don't, huh?

WATSON: It's just that they make me cough.

FRANK: You begrudge me makin' a livin'?

WATSON: You do all right.

FRANK: So everybody thinks.

WATSON: What's the matter?

FRANK: What do you care?

WATSON: You don't seem to be your jolly self.

FRANK: You ever feel like the old tricks aren't working?

WATSON: I was born feeling that way.

FRANK: Like a monkey on a chain dancing for apathetic children.

WATSON: Poor little monkey.

FRANK: I'm suffering, Watson.

WATSON: From what?

FRANK: Well. In a few words. I'm a very social person and I feel isolated.

WATSON: OK. I see. So you're down.

FRANK: Exactly! I'm down, Watson. I'm as down as I've ever been, and I hate it. I prefer to be happy. Well, what the hell is that? Who doesn't want to be happy?

WATSON: Lots of people.

FRANK: Really? Why?

WATSON: Otherwise engaged.

FRANK: And then there's my weight.

WATSON: You look fine.

FRANK: I'm fat. Wherever I go, I'm the fattest person in the room.

WATSON: A few pounds is all.

FRANK: I used to be as slinky as a puma. It's all part of the depression.

WATSON: Is that why you took to drugs?

FRANK: Why do you go right to that? I've cleaned up. Been through the Program three and a half times. *(Frank pops a pill.)*

WATSON: What's that you just took?

FRANK: Psychopharmaceutical.

WATSON: What's it do?

FRANK: Do I look like a M.D.? Goddam it, you've gotta have some faith, Watson! How 'bout a slice of lemon? *(Watson goes off for lemon.)* This atmosphere of cynicism is killing me! It's not just you. It's the attitude on every park bench. Look at me. I got something better to offer, but the problem is: It seems like nobody wants it. *(Watson reenters with lemon.)*

WATSON: You mean cigarettes?

FRANK: No! I'm talkin' about something intangible and fine. I'm talkin' about my heart. I'm talkin' about my soul. You know what I'm talking about? I'm talkin' about my philosophy.

WATSON: I didn't even know you had a philosophy.

FRANK: How do you think I became a success? It's because I operate from a philosophy.

WATSON: Well, what is it?

FRANK: Me. My philosophy is me. I believe I'm the best so that's what I sell. My message is simple: Be like me. Do like I do. And it works. I'm an idea, I put that idea out there, and people like the idea. The only problem is: People don't like me. They like the idea of me, they try to do like I do, but when they come face-to-face with the original article, their smile goes crocodile. The upshot? Well, take a gander. I'm alone. Success, yes. But what friends I have are bought and paid for. Nobody just likes me.

WATSON: What about your cronies?

FRANK: A man wearies of cronies.

WATSON: Well, I like you. Lots of people like you.

FRANK: I don't feel it.

WATSON: You want love.

FRANK: That's it. I want love, and nobody loves me.

WATSON: Can't help you there.

FRANK: Why not?

WATSON: It's not that I don't admire you, Frank. I do. I'd like to be you. I'd like to be sitting where you are, and you going about serving me.

FRANK: Well, that's how it was when I was a kid, remember? I used to sweep up and you'd be reading the paper.

WATSON: Those were the days. I thought they'd never end. Why did they end?

FRANK: I remember why. It's the day I made that cup a tea, and you charged me twice.

WATSON: I didn't charge you twice. Up until that point, I'd been giving us both the company discount. That day I decided to retain the discount for management, and abolish the discount for labor. You took it all wrong.

FRANK: It was unfair.

WATSON: Haven't you ever done anything unfair?

FRANK: Not that I like to remember.

WATSON: You overreacted.

FRANK: I by God stood up and took my place at table. I love you, Watson, but you're a son of a bitch when you've got the whip.

WATSON: Who isn't?

FRANK: Me.

WATSON: Hubris. First step on the slippery slope.

FRANK: You're right and I hear ya. That's why it's so good having you around.

WATSON: The voice of experience.

FRANK: Why, I can look at your face and see every mistake I might ever make.

WATSON: That's me. I'm a cautionary tale.

FRANK: You're a tonic is what you are! Just lookin' at the second-rate state you're in gives me a boost!

WATSON: We have a bond.

FRANK: That's right! Goddamn it, we do have a bond! We have a special relationship. *(Pulls out a pistol, hands it over to Watson.)* Here. What do you think a that shootin' stick? It's a beauty, ain't it?

WATSON: I can't afford to buy any more guns from you, Frank. I still owe you for the car.

FRANK: You love that car though, don't ya?

WATSON: It is a treat.

FRANK: Just feel the action.

WATSON: Why, when you're anxious, do you always resort to the sales pitch?

FRANK: Careful now. My daddy always said: "Guns are like Irishmen. Assume they're loaded." *(Watson has a good laugh.)*

WATSON: Ah, I do love a joke at the expense of the Irish. It is a nice little gun. Take it back. *(Watson puts the gun down.)*

FRANK: You don't have to pay me anytime soon. Shit, you don't have to pay me at all. Not in money anyways.

WATSON: Then how?

FRANK: I don't know. Wash my back sometimes.

WATSON: I can't make up my mind about you.

FRANK: How so?

WATSON: Faust or the Devil? *(Frank puts the gun in Watson's hand during the next line.)*

FRANK: Either way, we're in business. *(Indicating gun.)* Man, you look good with that iron Marlboro in your hand. You look like me. Wyatt Earp always said: "When you reach for a weapon and it ain't there, it's too late."

WATSON: Did Wyatt Earp really say that?

FRANK: Who cares? He's dead. Why don't you put that little piece a punctuation where you can reach it, if and when, so's you don't get caught short.

WATSON: All right. Better safe than sorry I suppose. *(Watson stows the pistol under the bar.)*

FRANK: That's the way. Deal done. Nothin's quite got the snap of a good transaction. What do you think? You want me to stand you to a drink? C'mon, I'll buy you a drink. *(Frank is about to pour a shot. Watson blocks the glass with his palm.)*

WATSON: I can't have a drink. I'd lose me job.

FRANK: Right. I did make that rule, and it is a good rule. But if I don't buy you a drink, maybe you'll start to hate me.

WATSON: You're so insecure.

FRANK: Wouldn't you be? No roots. Born in an orphanage. Everybody's child, nobody's son. That's my birth scar.

WATSON: What do you give a damn what other people think of you?

FRANK: What do they think of me?

WATSON: Who?

FRANK: Well, like your buddies.

WATSON: Oh, they think you're all right.

FRANK: No, they don't! Just all right, huh?

WATSON: Well, the Frenchman, he's never going to get on with you.

FRANK: Louie? Why not?

WATSON: He thinks you're gauche.

FRANK: Gauche.

WATSON: Go on. Ask me what it means.

FRANK: I don't care what it means.

WATSON: It means you're an awkward, embarrassing, clumsy person.

FRANK: Oh I am, huh? You know that a amphibian wants to eat like me, dress like me, and drive an SUV! And when the hell's he gonna give up speakin' French anyway?

WATSON: It's his language.

FRANK: It's pretentious. You don't speak in French.

WATSON: That's true.

FRANK: But you oughta lose that accent. You can if you put your mind to it. Practice speakin' like me.

WATSON: Take my advice. Don't bother about Louie. He's just jealous. There's nothing you can do about that.

FRANK: But I want him to like me!

WATSON: Why?

FRANK: I don't know. I wanna shine. That's the way I am. I wanna shine. So maybe I try too hard. Try to win everybody over. Try and try. But then I gotta tell you, this other thing kicks in, and I get full-up disgusted. Hate everybody. I think: Fuck 'em all. Who needs 'em? I go to my apartment, shut the door. Keep to myself. And cook. That's my passion.

WATSON: I didn't know that. You're a cook?

FRANK: I have to cook 'cause I love to eat. You know what the key to cooking is? Ingredients.

WATSON: Do you know what the problem with eating is: The more you eat, the more you want to eat.

FRANK: I give up cigarettes. I'm off the drugs. I gotta have something.

WATSON: When are you going to sit down with yourself and address your restless soul?

FRANK: Never. Sometimes I have a moment when this silence wraps itself around me like an anaconda. And I feel the Hate out there. I look up to the sky for comfort and see the majority is darkness and cold, and that the stars are ignorant and do not care. And that, that's when I have a major chow down. And as I eat my way to that latest plateau of satiety, the loneliness fades to gold. It's a new day. And I begin to fantasize about what the world COULD be. Don't you sometimes wish we could all sit down and bare our souls and get to some kind of deeper understanding?

WATSON: No.

FRANK: You don't?

WATSON: No.

FRANK: But how could you not want that, Watson?

WATSON: Well, to begin with, it would ruin the poker game.

FRANK: I don't even like poker.

WATSON: You can't kid me. You invented poker. There's that woman again.

FRANK: Who?

WATSON: There's this woman been looking in the window the last few days, but she never comes in.

FRANK: Jesus.

WATSON: What?

FRANK: I know her. Have you ever had a woman where you didn't know where to put her in your head? Where there's a chemistry so intense you can't afford to fuck her and you'd die if you cut her loose?

WATSON: I kind of feel that way about the Queen.

FRANK: She is like a Queen this one, a Queen in trouble, like some Cleopatra. But she's also something altogether new. A new kind of monarch brought to flower in the blood-soaked garden of world guilt. She's a dream, a folktale, her existence justified by prophecies and firepower. A thousand rivers from a hundred countries feed the headwaters of her soul. She's inevitable, impossible, the embodiment of Justice done. I'm telling you, the gods themselves fall back in fear that the hand of man has occasionally forged such a one as this. For when you make an ideal real, the blood will spill like adolescent tears. Is there anything more dangerous than a dream literally realized? Is there anything more . . . Romantic?

EVOLUTION
Jonathan Marc Sherman

Comic
Henry and Ernie, twenties

> *Henry is an academic type, pretty much clueless about anything hav-ing to do with popular culture. Ernie, his girlfriend Hope's brother, thinks Henry should forget about the thesis he is writing on Charles Darwin and do something meaningful with his life, like writing for TV.*

HENRY: Hey.

ERNIE: Hey. What are you doing up?

HENRY: Couldn't sleep. Had this . . . *dream.*

ERNIE: Did you nocturnally emit?

HENRY: Huh?

ERNIE: Did you jizz all over your boxers?

HENRY: No, no. It wasn't that kind of dream. It's just . . . I keep having it, and I can never get back to sleep afterwards.

ERNIE: Take a hit. It'll relax you.

HENRY: You think so?

ERNIE: I myself feel . . . pretty relaxed at this moment in time. Puffing. Watching some high-quality, top-of-the-line animation. It's extraor-dinarily relaxing.

HENRY: Thanks. *(Henry sits down next to Ernie, takes the joint, and smokes it. The two of them sit silently watching television, passing the joint back and forth between them.)* I think it's working. *(Beat.)* Who is that?

ERNIE: Who? The cartoon?

HENRY: Yeah.

ERNIE: Shut up.

HENRY: What?

ERNIE: You're not serious?

HENRY: I just asked who it was.

ERNIE: Have you ever seen that character before?

HENRY: Not that I'm aware of.

ERNIE: You're shitting me.

HENRY: I wouldn't shit you.

ERNIE: The dog biting the coin?

HENRY: Yeah.

ERNIE: You don't know who that dog is?

HENRY: No.

ERNIE: That's *Underdog.*

HENRY: Oh.

ERNIE: You mean to tell me you grew up in the United States of America and you don't recognize Underdog?

HENRY: I guess not.

ERNIE: You're a *freak,* Henry. *(Beat.)* I like that.

HENRY: I'm . . . really kind of . . . *high.*

ERNIE: I like that, too.

HENRY: *(Beat.)* That's *really* good pot.

ERNIE: My friend Marlon grew it. I'll pass your compliments along.

HENRY: Please do. *(Pause.)* I feel like I'm — *(Exhales.)* — very quiet . . . *drifting* . . . drifting . . . *(Ernie takes a bottle of pills out of his pocket, opens it, and hands a pill to Henry, along with his soda.)*

ERNIE: Yeah, well, before you drift completely into nothingness and disappear, Underdog, I think you should take this.

HENRY: What is it?

ERNIE: *Methampex.*

HENRY: Oh. *(Henry takes the pill and washes it down with soda while Ernie nonchalantly flips the television channels so there are different images on each television; an infomercial, a music video, a test pattern, a religion show, and an old sitcom. Beat.)* What's Methampex?

ERNIE: Anti-disappearant.

HENRY: Huh?

ERNIE: So you don't disappear.

HENRY: So . . . I won't disappear?

ERNIE: On the contrary. You will now *appear.*

HENRY: *(Beat.)* I don't get it.

ERNIE: It's Desoxyn.

HENRY: I still don't get it.

ERNIE: High-quality, blue-ribbon *speed.*

HENRY: *(Beat.)* Speed?

ERNIE: Speed.

HENRY: I've never done speed.

ERNIE: That's no longer true.

HENRY: Isn't it fairly dangerous?

ERNIE: Being *alive* can be fairly dangerous, Henry.

HENRY: Yes, but isn't speed specifically, especially dangerous?

ERNIE: Well, yes, Henry, it can be. It most certainly can be. I mean, let's face it, anything that makes your brain and body feel like staying energetically awake for long periods of times without nourishment is probably not the healthiest or most organic choice to make in the long run. But you know what rule I live my life by, Henry?

HENRY: What's that?

ERNIE: *Moderation.* In all things. I mean, if just a couple of pills could kill you, doctors probably wouldn't be able to prescribe them.

HENRY: Doctors *prescribe* speed?

ERNIE: Doctors prescribe *Methampex.* For people who are troubled by *extreme* obesity. Now, you and I are *not* troubled by extreme obesity, Henry, and we should be thankful for that, and try to enjoy our speediness while it lasts. Don't you think?

HENRY: I *think* I should have Just Said No.

ERNIE: All of that Just-Say-No crap has been severely misinterpreted. People miss the whole beauty of the thing. Just *Say* No. All you have to do is *say* it. You can still *do* drugs. Watch, I'll do a demonstration for you. *(Shakes his head.)* No. *(Takes a pill and washes it down with soda, shakes his head again.)* No . . . I'm sorry, but . . . *No. (Ernie takes another pill and washes it down with soda. From this point on, the scene moves quickly.)* See how easy that was, Henry? Actions speak louder than words. Kind of a stupid expression, actually. If actions speak louder than words, why would anybody *say* "Actions speak louder than words"?

HENRY: I don't know, Ernie.

ERNIE: *Henry.* I don't *care* if actions speak louder than words. I'm going to say a couple of words to you, so look into my eyes. *(Beat.) Trust me. (Beat.)* OK? Trust me, Henry. You'll be OK, but you've got to trust me, because without trust, human beings might as well be plastic drinking straws.

HENRY: *(Beat.)* Plastic drinking straws?

ERNIE: OK, OK, OK, bad example. *(Beat.)* The smallest human being ever, Henry, was a full-grown woman under two feet tall. You know how small that is? *(Indicates with his hand.)* Very fucking small. And she wasn't a G.I. Joe, or some Cabbage Patch thing, she was a woman, with a brain and a body and emotions and a spine, OK? Imagine if she was in this room with us, you know, you'd stare at her, and she could look back at you, and talk to you, and maybe even fall in love with you. Less than two feet tall, Henry. Not big. And every moment of her life, she had to completely trust the people around her, because she had no choice. *(Beat.) All* of us are her, Henry, we're *all* less than two feet tall, and unless we put ourselves into the hands of others, we don't add up to jack shit, so *Trust Me.*

HENRY: *(Beat.)* I feel a little better, now that you took two.

ERNIE: Side by side, Henry. I'm a firm believer in the power of teamwork. Moderation and teamwork, those are the linchpins of my existence — motherfucking-fucking-fucking-*fuck!*

HENRY: Oh, no.

ERNIE: Those guys are bullshit! They're hacks!

HENRY: What guys?

ERNIE: On the TV screen.

HENRY: *Which* TV screen?

ERNIE: The one in the middle. The music video guys. The so-called musicians on the middle TV.

HENRY: What's wrong with them?

ERNIE: Oh, come *on,* Henry. My band made these guys look like they were all still in grade school, playing the *recorder.*

HENRY: You're in a band?

ERNIE: Yeah, I'm in a Goddamn *band. (Ernie turns off the televisions.)* I mean, not anymore, we broke up, I quit. We had a great concept, all hard-core Bee Gees covers, but we had a shitty look, we clearly weren't going anyplace.

HENRY: That's too bad.

ERNIE: Also, everybody was addicted to heroin.

HENRY: Oh.

ERNIE: Except for me. But, you know, I come in, completely speedy all the time, wanting to play, play, play, everybody else was just sitting around all the time, staring at their instruments. Not a good mix. Listen to me. Sound like a schoolmarm. "Not a good mix." You want to know what it really was. It was *Clash of the Titans.* You saw that. *(Beat.)* Henry?

HENRY: What?

ERNIE: You saw *Clash of the Titans?*

HENRY: No.

ERNIE: With Laurence Olivier?

HENRY: No.

ERNIE: Olivier was a serious badass madman performer. You see *Marathon Man?*

HENRY: No.

ERNIE: Olivier played this Nazi dentist asking Tootsie if it's safe, freaking me out, I'm saying to myself, Grandpa Olivier might as well call it quits and retire, 'cause how can you top a *Nazi dentist?* So what does he go and do? He plays *Zeus.* The Big Guy. The god of gods. *Clash of the Titans.* Some powerful stuff, my friend, makes you think, myths and shit. You ever study myths at school?

HENRY: Not really.

ERNIE: But that's what you're *supposed* to study at school. What do you study instead of myths?

HENRY: Uhh, Darwin, mostly. I spend most of my time studying . . . *Darwin.*

ERNIE: Darwin. *(Beat.)* Huh. *(Beat.)* I keep trying to convince Dad to give me the cash he'd waste if I actually decided to spend four years playing at college. I could put a hundred grand in the bank, collect some interest, you know, live a free life, read, talk to people, hang out with my friends — the basic college thing, just keep the cash for some security down the line.

HENRY: College sucks.

ERNIE: *(Beat.)* What was that?

HENRY: College really sucks.

ERNIE: I can't believe I'm hearing this. Aren't you Mister Doctorate Grad School, intelligent young man dating my older sister? Doesn't sound like the kind of guy who'd say "College sucks."

HENRY: I mean it.

ERNIE: If it sucks, what are you doing? Getting your Doctorate in Doggy Paddling? Time is short, my friend.

HENRY: Time isn't short or long, it's just time.

ERNIE: And it's *ticking*. It doesn't stop while you're getting your diploma, your $100,000 paper airplane. Time's like a car with a self-refilling gas tank.

HENRY: Great simile, Ernie. Real strong.

ERNIE: I'm serious, man. I was flipping through *Playboy* the other day —

HENRY: For the articles, right?

ERNIE: No, for the airbrushed pictures of women's tits. I'm reading the Playmate Questionnaire in the middle, you know, because I'm really interested to know what her favorite books are, and look at her date of birth, and . . . she was born in '83. *(Beat.) Nineteen*-eighty-three. That's a landmark in a man's life, the first time you're older than the *Playboy* centerfold. No more kid stuff. The time for action is *now*. You feel alive?

HENRY: Yeah, yeah. I do.

ERNIE: That's the speed. *(Beat.)* They asked my girlfriend to pose for *Playboy*. She told them to suck her dick. *(Beat.)* Just an expression, of course, she's not a hermaphrodite or anything. *(Takes a picture from his wallet and shows it to Henry.)* That's her.

HENRY: She looks beautiful.

ERNIE: She's a bitch.

HENRY: Why are you dating her, then?

ERNIE: I love carrying her picture in my wallet. It's a great photo. But in person, it's all confrontational bullshit, nagging, she wants *this,* so that means I can't do *that,* all sorts of fenced-in feelings. Who needs it? I mean, don't get me wrong, I still get together with her. You can't fuck a picture, you know what I'm saying? Unless you're some perverse sicko cutting holes with scissors and you know, God bless, live and let live, that's not up my alley, I prefer living, breathing flesh. You can keep your two-dimensional photographic representations and blow-up plastic dolls, thank you very much, sorry, no sale, you know?

HENRY: Uh-huh.

ERNIE: *(Beat.)* So, you keep a snapshot of my sis in your wallet?

HENRY: Huh?

ERNIE: You got a photo of Hope in your billfold?

HENRY: Oh. Oh, no. No, she says photographs steal your soul.

ERNIE: That's not what she said when she was thirteen. She went off to college a sister, she comes back an Indian chief. Photographs steal your soul. Come on, Hope, it's the twenty-first century, time to take off the hoop skirt. *(Beat.)* You got a charcoal *sketch* of her in your wallet?

HENRY: Nope. Just this. *(Henry takes a picture from his wallet and shows it to Ernie.)*

ERNIE: Who's this? Grandpa?

HENRY: That's Charles Darwin.

ERNIE: Oh. *(Beat.)* Could've used a Mach III, know what I'm saying? *(Beat.)* You know, actually, if you get rid of the beard and the moustache, then weave all that facial hair onto the top of his head . . . I swear to Christ, that's incredible.

HENRY: What?

ERNIE: If Charles Darwin shaved and joined Hair Club for Men, he'd be the spitting image of Aaron Spelling.

HENRY: Who's Aaron Spelling?

ERNIE: Oh, Henry, baby, you're killing me. Aaron Spelling is legendary. *The Love Boat, Fantasy Island . . . 90210, Melrose Place, Charmed, Seventh Heaven, Dynasty . . . Charlie's Angels.* Aaron Spelling. He's like a living TV *god.* How can you not know Aaron Spelling? Or *Clash of the Titans?* Or Underdog? It's like you were raised by wolves or — Whoa. *(Beat.)* Stop. *(Beat.) Stop. (Beat.)* Oh, yeah. Oh, *yeah.*

HENRY: Oh, yeah *what?*

ERNIE: Shut up for a second, Henry. It's all coming together, making sense, fortifying — I'm going to say a couple of words to you, so look into my eyes. *(Beat.) Fuck Edison. (Beat.)* Was that clear? Should I repeat it? I *will* repeat it. *Fuck Edison.* Do you know what that means?

HENRY: I don't think so.

ERNIE: It means . . . exactly what it sounds like. Fuck Edison. You see.

HENRY: Not . . . *really* . . .

ERNIE: Fuck Edison and his 99 percent perspiration, 1 percent inspiration malarkey, because perspiration is sweat and inspiration is genius, and I rank genius far above sweat, so . . . *hence* . . . *Fuck Edison.* Is it all becoming as clear to you as it is to me?

HENRY: I'm trying to put it all together with you, Ernie, but —

ERNIE: OK, look: Moderation; Teamwork; The *Playboy* Doggy Paddling Theory; and Fucking Edison. Those are the four basic food groups that fuel my every waking moment. And for some unknown reason — call it *fate,* Henry, call it *kismet* — all of my major concepts have merged to point me in the direction of the ultimate paradise that is going to be our collective future. *(Beat.)* I'm a Johnny-on-the-spot kind of guy, Henry, I may seem lazy, but I know when the time is ripe, and Henry, right now, the clockworks are *dripping. (Beat.)* Darwin's basic gist was that we descend with modifications along the way, right?

HENRY: How did you know that?

ERNIE: Surprise, surprise, Henry. I was extremely well-educated when I was a small child, I just fucked it all up as I got taller. I know some handy tidbits of information, but I'm certainly no scholar. You, on the other hand, the left hand, since I was just gesticulating with my right hand, you, Henry, you certainly *are* a scholar. Pump it up, Henry. Use what you've learned. Darwin talked about adaptation, right? *Adapt.* Grow. Change. Look around, see what's going on, and realize the classroom is outdated, it's no longer the place for you. Harvard may have been exciting once, brand-new, then it matured, but now . . . now, Henry, now it's *traditional. Harvard.* It's old news. I mean, what if the Brat Pack kept clinging to *St. Elmo's Fire,* Henry? Huh? Tell me. What *if?*

HENRY: *(Beat.)* What is *St. Elmo's Fire?*

ERNIE: Ask Rob Lowe. *(Beat.)* Don't tell me . . . you know who Rob Lowe is, don't you?

HENRY: The name sounds vaguely familiar.

ERNIE: *(Beat.)* Henry, you're a *tabula rasa* sent to me by the gods to alter television and change *history. Adapt.* Adapt and *Plunge.*

HENRY: *(Beat.)* Ernie?

ERNIE: *Yes?*

HENRY: What the *fuck* are you talking about? *(Ernie gestures grandly to the televisions.)*

ERNIE: *TV!*

HENRY: What about it?

ERNIE: That's where we belong. That's where we're going to go. I've got a friend whose father's a network hotshot. He can pull some strings, get us in the *door.*

HENRY: You're evidently excited, Ernie, I'm aware of that, I get that. But, what . . . what *door* do we need to get *in?*

ERNIE: The television network door. How can I make you understand, Henry? *Darwin's* door. When he wrote about survival of the fittest and reproduction. Darwin was writing about TV. Charles Darwin is alive and well and living in Southern California, Henry. Aaron Spelling is the reincarnation of Charles Darwin. Take *Charlie's Angels.* A TV show about three beautiful women detectives, a show that not only survived on television, a show that *prospered.* These women were *fit,* Henry, the *fittest,* and TV reproduced them over and over and over, ad infinitum . . . ad nauseam . . . with ads in between to sell products that consumers don't actually want or need. But we're not going to be consumers, Henry. We're going to penetrate the shell of that angelic machine that is TV. Talk about *affecting* people. TV. Everybody has it, everybody watches it.

HENRY: I don't.

ERNIE: That's the *point.* You don't know what you're doing, so you'll have fresh ideas, and that's what TV needs, all the time, it's like a vampire in need of blood. *We're* the blood, Henry.

HENRY: We are?

ERNIE: Yes, we are. And if our blood type is their blood type, they pay *Big.* Bigger than the Red Cross. *So* much bigger than the Red Cross. TV makes the Red Cross look *this* big, Henry, *this* big — *(Gestures with his fingers.)* — *Tiny.* The Red Cross is a trinket some kid with sticky elbows wears on a chain around his neck. TV — *TV,* Henry, TV is this gargantuan crucifix with all civilization nailed to it, hook, line, sinker — there ain't nobody getting off this baby, Henry. And just think . . . we can be a part of it. I keep you pumped up, juices flowing, you write the damn words down — WHIZ — BANG — we've got a script and we're in the door. We're in the foyer of the whole damn *thing!*

HENRY: You want me to write *scripts?*

ERNIE: You got it!

HENRY: Ernie, the only things I've ever written are critical term papers at school.

ERNIE: Words are words.

HENRY: I think I get it. You want us to write TV shows?

ERNIE: No, I *need* us to write TV shows.

HENRY: You seem to have a flair for the dramatic. Why don't you do it yourself?

ERNIE: What's my most important rule, Henry?

HENRY: Moderation?

ERNIE: *Teamwork.* Simon and Garfunkel. Jekyll and Hyde. Ernie and Bert.

HENRY: Who's Bert?

ERNIE: From *Sesame Street.*

HENRY: Where the hell is *Sesame Street?*

ERNIE: You are so *untainted.* So *pure.* That's our selling point. You've been living like a monk in the trenches of academia preparing for this task. You haven't gotten your finger on the pulse of the American public, Henry, you've got your finger on the pulse of *All Civilization,* from the Big Bang to Evolution. I see it now: *Evolution — The Television Event of All Time.* Written by You. Executive Produced by Me. Created by Us. Me and You. The Spark and the Follow-Through. The Quirk and the Rock.

HENRY: *(Beat.)* What does an executive producer *do?*

ERNIE: I keep you happy and bank my rather excessive paycheck *daily. (Beat.)* But it's not about the money, Henry. I mean, the money's gonna be nice, but it's not what it's *about.* It's about the *power.* The feeling that you can only get when you're tuned into *everything,* when your ideas and your creation are being pumped into the minds of people *everywhere. (Beat.)* Take Madonna, for instance. She's used music and videos and the press to her advantage and created an *empire.* She's changed the course of *history,* influenced the entire *world. (Beat.)* Do you know who Madonna is, Henry?

HENRY: Yeah, I know Madonna.

ERNIE: See what I'm saying, Henry? Even *you* know Madonna. I guarantee you I can find Madonna somewhere on television right this very second. *(Ernie flips the channels on one of the televisions until he finds Madonna singing the song "Holiday" in concert, from the movie* Truth or Dare. *When he does, he flips the channels on the rest of the televisions to that station, so the Madonna video is on all five televisions. There is a long pause as Ernie and Henry stare at the televisions. Long pause.)* We can be everywhere, Henry. Not just right here, right now. Everywhere. For All Time. *(The lights blackout. The Madonna video ends. Title:* Femme Fatale Flash Cards. *Gina appears in a spotlight, holding flash cards.)*

GINA: *What German singer-actress said, "It's the friends you can call at four in the morning that really matter"? (Beat.)* Marlene Dietrich. *(Checks the back of the card.) What pop culture sensation wrote, "I love my pussy. I think it's a complete summation of my life"? (Beat.)* Madonna. *(Gina checks the back of the card as the light on her fades. The hallway. Ernie is standing outside the bathroom door. We can't see Henry, who's inside the bathroom, getting ready.)*

ERNIE: Nonalcoholic beer. *(Beat.)* Henry?

HENRY: *(Offstage.)* Yeah?

ERNIE: Hear what I'm saying?

HENRY: *(Offstage.)* Uh-huh.

ERNIE: I mean, nonalcoholic *beer?* *(Beat.)* What the *hell?* What's the point? Who thinks these things up? BING, idea, lightbulb on the scalp, I got it, hold the press, nonalcoholic beer! It's like, you know, I'm like, fuck you, buddy, ever hear of ginger *ale?* Get a *job. (Beat.)* Henry?

HENRY: *(Offstage.)* Yeah?

ERNIE: How's it coming, how you doing, what's happening in there, you almost set?

HENRY: *(Offstage.)* Almost.

ERNIE: You need help with anything? Knotting your tie or anything?

HENRY: *(Offstage.)* I think I've got it.

ERNIE: I'm telling you, funny thing about ties, they save an hour of making good impressions with these kind of guys. Men with jobs like men with ties. There's no way around it. It's just an indisputable kind of fact and you either roll with it or go into the wilderness and never be heard from again. *(Beat.)* You know what's a sensational thing, Henry?

HENRY: *(Offstage.)* What?

ERNIE: Not nonalcoholic beer — but *plums. (Beat.)* I'm a little, you know, antsy. *(Beat.)* Big Day, Big Day. *(Beat.)* Shouldn't take it out on you, misplaced angst, not good, not healthy, not productive, not a step in the staircase — Jesus, listen to me, Little Miss Muffet. Tuffet. Curds. Whey. You must think I'm scattered. I'm not scattered, Henry, just getting pumped up, and, you know, so that gets me a little scattery. That's OK. *(Beat.)* That's OK, Henry, isn't it?

HENRY: *(Offstage.)* Fine.

ERNIE: Good. *(Beat.)* You have a burning desire to do something, you work out a realistic plan, you come to terms with what you're willing to lose to get what you want — Home Free. *(Beat.) Marco.*

HENRY: *(Offstage. Beat.)* Polo.

ERNIE: Marco.

HENRY: *(Offstage.)* Polo.

ERNIE: *Ha.* Teamwork, Henry, we play off each other well, teamwork. *(Beat.)* What am I, sitting here, twiddling my thumbs, playing kiddy games, *testing.* Henry, you think we're gonna be great today?

HENRY: *(Offstage.)* Yeah.

ERNIE: You do? You excited.

HENRY: *(Offstage.)* Sure, yeah.

ERNIE: I'm excited, too, Henry, I'm — Henry, I'm putting my fists on my chest and moving them rapidly up and down, my heart's pumping blood into my hair, I think we're gonna blow these network suits away.

HENRY: *(Offstage.)* Me, too.

ERNIE: Just remember this, Henry. We gotta get the essence of things, Henry, get to the core, strip away the bullshit. We're going to take this town, this *world,* and we're gonna *digest* it. You and I, Henry, you and I are gonna make the Backstreet Boys look like Herman's Hermits.

FISHER KING
Don Nigro

Dramatic
Rudd and Perce, twenties

> *Rudd, a young Union soldier, sits by his campfire one dark night toward the end of the American Civil War, alone in the dark woods, his gun apart, cleaning it. He's deserted in order to find and kill the person who had sex with his sister Bel on a pump organ in his father's revival tent. Sound of someone thrashing about in the bushes. Perce, a backwoods boy who wants to be a soldier, stumbles awkwardly into the light, with his own gun. Knowing that Perce is the one he's been looking for, Rudd tries to put his gun back together as calmly and patiently as possible, before Perce figures out that Rudd knows what he did to Rudd's sister.*

PERCE: Hi. It's OK. I'm friendly. I didn't mean to sneak up on you.

RUDD: Boy, you couldn't sneak up on a rock. You got a elephant back there with you, or what?

PERCE: No. I don't think so.
(Perce stands a little ways from the campfire, uncertain.)
It's cold tonight.
(Rudd continues putting his gun back together, says nothing.)
You mind if I join you?

RUDD: Suit yourself. What you doin' way out here in the middle of the woods, boy? Snipe huntin'?

PERCE: *(Moving closer to the fire.)* Gone to enlist. Fight for the Union Army. But they keep movin' around on me.

RUDD: Scared of you, I reckon.

PERCE: Hey, I know you. You're the one came by my ma's house with Major Pendragon. You on leave or somethin'?

RUDD: Sure. Major sent me on special leave, said I deserve it for bein' such a good soldier. Gave me a big kiss good-bye, then he cried a whole bunch into his hanky.

PERCE: Is that a fact? You got a drink of water? I'm awful thirsty.

RUDD: Canteen right over there.

PERCE: Thank you kindly. *(Perce puts his gun down, goes to the canteen, picks it up, unscrews the cap.)* I guess my mama was right. Throw your bread in the creek and it'll float back to you downstream.

RUDD: Come again?

PERCE: We give you water, and now you give me water. Funny how things work out like that. I mean, you look all over for somethin', and just when you're about to give up on it, damn if it don't drop right in your lap. *(Perce drinks.)*

RUDD: *(Trying not to show how anxious he is to get the gun back together, or how angry he is.)* Ain't that amazing.

PERCE: Where you headed?

RUDD: Goin' to visit my sister.

PERCE: Is that right? She live around here?

RUDD: You familiar with these woods?

PERCE: Kind of. Not exactly. I get lost a lot.

RUDD: Funniest thing just happened to me. I come across this old guy fishin' in the creek, back there a ways, in the deepest part of the woods, and he asked me to come back to his house so I could meet his daughter. Big white house, he said.

PERCE: Sounds good to me. Big white house?

RUDD: Yep.

PERCE: Around here?

RUDD: That's what he said.

PERCE: Did you go?

RUDD: No, I didn't.

PERCE: Why not? If that'd been me, I'd have taken him right up on that offer. I mean, that would sound to me like a nice opportunity, man with a big white house, meet his daughter. Why didn't you go?

RUDD: I got somethin' else to do first.

(The gun is back together now. Rudd is loading it.)

PERCE: Yeah? What's that?

RUDD: See, I been lookin' for this fella.

PERCE: What fella?

RUDD: Fella I know.

PERCE: Why's that?

RUDD: Well, I got a present for him, you see.

PERCE: What kind of present?

RUDD: This fella I'm lookin' for, see, big dumb kid from the hills, not far
from here, he did something to my sister.

PERCE: Your sister?

RUDD: Yeah. On her organ. By my daddy's tent. And when I find this boy,
you know what I'm gonna do?

PERCE: *(Canteen still in his hand, looking at his own gun on the ground.)*
No. What?

RUDD: I'm gonna put his head on a stick, take it back to his ma's place,
and plant it in the front yard.

PERCE: Is that a fact? Well, look, I hope you find this feller you're lookin
for, and I thank you kindly for the water, but I got to be on my way
now.

RUDD: You know a boy like that, do a thing like that?

PERCE: No, I can't say as I do. *(Perce puts the canteen down and reaches for
his gun, trying to be casual.)*

RUDD: *(Pointing his gun at Perce.)* Don't move, boy.
(Perce stops.)

RUDD: You're an awful stupid kid. You know that? You're probably the stu-
pidest damned son of a bitch I ever met, and I met some really stupid people in the Army. You know what I'm gonna do, after I put
your head on a stick, and plant it in your front yard? I'm gonna go
in your house and do to your ma what you done to my sister. And
I'm gonna tell her you sent me.

PERCE: Hey, now, listen here. You ain't got no call to talk about my ma
like that. I ain't never did nothin' to your sister.

RUDD: Tell Amos and Jack about it when you get to Hell, Jesus. The first
shot's goin to the crotch, I think.

PERCE: Hey. No. Hey, no, please, please, no. AHHHHHHHHHH.
*(Rudd pulls the trigger. Click. Nothing. He looks at the gun. Fires again.
Click.)*

RUDD: Shit. I musta left somethin' out again. Damn, I always do that. Where the hell is it?

(Rudd looks around for the missing part. Perce picks up his own gun, levels it at Rudd and pulls the trigger. Rudd lurches backwards from the impact, sprawls, writhes, stops. Pause. Sound of the fire. An owl. Fire shadows on Perce.)

PERCE: Just like shootin' squirrels. Nothin' to it. *(He stares at the body.)* You dead, or what? *(He pokes the body with his foot.)* Yeah, you're dead all right. *(He takes another drink from the canteen.)* You stop shakin' now, Perce. He shouldn't have said that about a person's mother. That ain't right. I sure like that red bandanna you got there. *(He takes the bandanna.)* Wash the blood off that, wear it when I'm a soldier, fight for Major Pendragon. I could use that coat, too. You sure don't need it no more. Good thing you didn't have it on, or it'd have a big old hole in it now, like you. And that hat. I can wash the blood out in the creek. I can just drag you in the bushes and leave you for the crows. Dead folks all over these woods. One more stiff ain't gonna make much difference. Hell, it ain't hard at all to be a soldier. Just like shootin' squirrels. It's just like shootin' squirrels.

FRIENDLY COMPETITION
Jesse Jamison

Comic

Baxter, twenty-something production executive, sworn nemesis of Jones
Jones, twenty-something production executive, sworn nemesis of Baxter

> *Baxter and Jones are rivals at the International N-Tertainment Com-*
> *pany, Inc. Constantly attaching each other to horrible projects in an*
> *attempt to cause the other to lose his job, Baxter has finally crossed*
> *the line. Jones is now stuck producing* Bible II: the Reckoning —
> *a sequel to the Bible based on the* Star Wars *trilogy. We pick up as*
> *Jones has finished reading this abysmal script.*

JONES: *(He stares at the audience with wide-open, horrified eyes.)* I'm going
to lose my job. *(Short pause.)* I haven't seen a script this bad since Baxter signed me up for "Schindler's *Shopping* List " — *(Pause — Real-
ization.)* Baxter. It's Baxter again! No way this script just happened
to float my way. He must be behind this. *(He moves to his desk, and
pushes a button on his phone.)* Well, I'm not letting him go this time.
(To Boss.) Uh, hey, Boss, this is Jones . . . anyway, I've decided to go
all out on this new project. *(Pause.)* Yeah, I've decided that I can't handle this alone. Would you mind letting me call in a favor? I need a
co-executive producer. *(Pause — then evilly.)* Baxter. Thanks. *(Hangs
up, chuckles malevolently.)* This should be fun. *(Sits in his swivel chair,
points at the door.)* Three, two, one . . .
BAXTER: *(Bursting in as Jones says "one.")* You son of a —
JONES: *(Cutting him off.)* Hi, Baxter!
BAXTER: This is unacceptable! Unacceptable!
JONES: What's unacceptable, Baxter? Is there something wrong?
BAXTER: Don't you play stupid with me, Jones. I invented that bit.
JONES: You know, I'd have to agree with you on that one.
BAXTER: *(Pause, then — to himself.)* Man, I set myself up for that. *(Then,*

to Jones.) Regardless! You know what I'm talking about. A sequel to the Bible that rips off *Star Wars?*

JONES: Oh, come on, Baxter. Who's playing stupid now? Cut the crap. I know you're behind this. No way could this script just *appear.*

BAXTER: All right, *maybe* I pulled some strings and got you put on this project. But to get *me* put on it? Please. That's just childish. I mean, I know we have this friendly competition —

JONES: *Friendly* competition? Baxter, you put me on *Alf-a-palooza 2000.* That was *malicious.*

BAXTER: *Alf* was malicious? This, coming from the guy who signed me up for *Friends on Ice?*

JONES: *(Chuckles happily and sighs.)* Yeah. *(Then, seriously.)* But seriously, Baxter. Did you actually read that script before you sent it my way?

BAXTER: Yeah. *(Jones looks at him.)* I skimmed it. *(Jones looks at him.)* Read the synopsis. *(Jones looks at him — Baxter hangs his head in shame.)* I had my secretary read the synopsis to me.

JONES: *(Closing the door.)* All right, Baxter, this is bigger than any of our paltry differences. I don't think I'm exaggerating when I say that this is quite possibly the most volatile movie premise of all time. This movie, improperly produced, could bring down this entire production company.

BAXTER: *(Leaning in, conspiratorially.)* You wanna take down the company?

JONES: No! I — *(Considering this.)* No! If we don't handle this properly, it's both our jobs. Like it or not, we're in this together now. You — and me. Let's face it, Baxter. We're the best there is. If we can't save this movie, then no one can. *(Smiling.)* And, should the movie flop, you'll get fired too. So, the way I look at it, I win either way.

BAXTER: You evil genius. But I do agree with you on one thing: I am more talented than you are.

JONES: That's not what I said.

BAXTER: You need me. I'll hear what I want to hear.

JONES: Fine, whatever.

BAXTER: That's what I thought. Now lets get hacking at this thing. How do you think we should market this movie?

JONES: I don't know. This one's going to be tricky. It takes itself just seriously enough that we can't make it look like a farce or a satirical comedy.

BAXTER: We could market it as an artistic movie.

JONES: Good point. I was thinking maybe as an art film, but frankly, it's the most offensive thing I've ever read, and I haven't been to church since the nineties.

BAXTER: It's that bad? It's stupid, but I didn't think it was *that* bad.

JONES: *(Holding up the script.)* Baxter, Jesus walks on water *using the Force.*

BAXTER: That's not so bad.

JONES: *(Glancing at the script.)* King Herod is a seven-hundred-pound demon named "Herod the Hutt."

BAXTER: *(Shuddering involuntarily, but still pushing his words through.)* It's not that bad.

JONES: *(Flips through the script.)* Jesus blows up the "Death Temple" with a "Torpedo of Faith."

BAXTER: All right, all right! Don't you think I can tell it's bad? *(They both pause, thinking.)* What are we going to do, Jones? We're in over our heads here.

JONES: Maybe we can call in the screenwriter? Do you think we could — we could get a re-write that was less offensive?

BAXTER: Maybe . . . let's set up a meeting with the guy.

JONES: I don't know — I'm kinda scared to meet him — I mean, what do you imagine when you think of a person who could possibly write a script *that* bad? *(Noticing the name on the script:)* By Knight Sunskimmer, priest of the Church of Reformed Jedi? *(A beat.)* We're going to lose our jobs.

. . . IN THE ABSENCE OF SPRING . . .

Joe Calarco

Dramatic
Jason, thirties; Marty, thirties

> *Jason, everyone's best friend but with lots of issues that he hides very well. Gay but not stereotypical. Marty, uncomplicated, straightforward, a waiter. Gay but not stereotypical: a guy's guy. Has sex, likes sex, talks about sex, and a real romantic. Believes in fate and the possibility of true love. Jason is waiting for a subway. Marty runs up.*

MARTY: Hey . . . Hey . . . You forgot your keys.

JASON: Incredible, to the rescue again.

MARTY: Look, I can take a hint. I can just disappear.

JASON: No, I have to find . . . it's not about you. Look, I had this — you wouldn't believe me even if I told you.

MARTY: Try me.

JASON: Fuck it's cold down here.

MARTY: Take my jacket.

JASON: What?

MARTY: I'm layered.

JASON: No.

MARTY: Really.

JASON: No.

MARTY: No big deal.

JASON: I can't.

MARTY: Really.

JASON: Hey, I could be like some psycho jacket hog.

MARTY: I'll get it back.

JASON: You will?

MARTY: Hey, undeniable things.

JASON: I'm talking, hoarding them.

MARTY: I mean, there is such a thing as chemistry.

JASON: Closets full.

MARTY: Animal scents. Secretions.

JASON: You know friends', strangers', any I can grab a hold of. It's like a fetish. Never returned. Jackets never seen again.

MARTY: I mean, fuck pondering. I just say, "Hey. Take me along." 'Cause some things are just like from — well, like farther back than us. It's in the — well, like in the dust we come from. I mean, there are some things you just know.

JASON: What?

MARTY: I usually, work nights, so —

JASON: What?

MARTY: Days are better for me.

JASON: What?

MARTY: So like maybe breakfast —

JASON: Marty —

MARTY: Though I'm more of a brunch person myself.

JASON: Look —

MARTY: You know, late nights —

JASON: Well, actually —

MARTY: Some times I'm just dragging —

JASON: I'm sorry Marty. I can't do this.

MARTY: What?

JASON: I . . . I just can't.

MARTY: What are you — . . . ?

JASON: I . . . I . . . this . . . I . . . ummm . . .

MARTY: Hey — . . .

JASON: I can't — . . . ummm . . .

MARTY: Jas.

JASON: There. See? See? I don't know you. I don't know you.

MARTY: Well, yeah, but we could —

JASON: No. See? "Jas." There it is. There it is.

MARTY: Come on. Let's grab a cup of —

JASON: Jas? You can't call me that. I don't give you permission to call me that.

MARTY: Well, I'm sorry, but —

JASON: No. No. *I'm* sorry. I can't. I can't. Not — not shortened names and sharing clothes and — once-a-week movies and twice-a-week dinners. Spending one night a week. Then two. Then three and — and spare toothbrushes and phone calls just to hear your voice —

MARTY: What are you —

JASON: — Sunday mornings in bed dreaming about our country house —

MARTY: What —

JASON: — Renting U-hauls and picking out curtains and buying matching dishes —

MARTY: Hey, hey —

JASON: — Housewarmings, year anniversaries, checking out adoption agencies for Christ's sake — !

MARTY: Can we just —

JASON: — Rolling around on the living room rug, laughing and arguing over who was the first to say "I love you."

MARTY: JASON!

JASON: Would you swallow my cum?

MARTY: What?

JASON: A year from now, if I came home with beer on my breath and the faint smell of another man's cologne on my skin, would you?

MARTY: I need you to —

JASON: No. I'm asking you. After rings, and commitment ceremonies, and six-month tests, and twelve-month tests. After two hours of "I'd never do that to you" and two hours of "I can't believe you'd think that" and two hours of "Don't you trust me?" and two hours of "I love you." After all that, would you swallow my cum?

MARTY: Umm . . . Uhhh . . . *(He cannot answer.)*

JASON: See? Trust? I mean *real* trust. It's become an impossible act. It has ceased to exist. So why bother? We all might just as well spend the rest of our lives alone.

(Marty leaves.)

. . . IN THE ABSENCE OF SPRING . . .

Joe Calarco

Dramatic
Jason, thirties; Jimmy

> *Jason, everyone's best friend but with lots of issues that he hides very well. Gay but not stereotypical. Jimmy is Jason's boyfriend who died seven years before. Jason has somehow fantastically returned to the place where Jimmy died in Scotland. Though Jimmy is an apparition, he is very, very real. Jason is in a field. He hears a voice but does not know where it is coming from.*

JIMMY: Jason?
JASON: Hello?!
JIMMY: Jason.
JASON: Who — ?
JIMMY: Jason.
JASON: Who's there?
JIMMY: Jas, it's me.
JASON: Who?
JIMMY: Remember me?
JASON: Oh my God.
JIMMY: Jas.
JASON: Oh my God.
JIMMY: Jas.
JASON: Oh my God . . .
JIMMY: Jas, it's really me.
　　(Jimmy appears.)
JASON: Jimmy?
JIMMY: Surprise.
JASON: Jimmy?

JIMMY: In the flesh — spiritually speaking.

JASON: But . . . But you — . . . How can — ? How — . . . This — This — This can't — It can't —

JIMMY: You look tired.

JASON: *(Laugh.)* Jesus . . .

JIMMY: You should get out more.

JASON: This is insane . . . This is —

JIMMY: Have some fun.

JASON: What is happening here?

JIMMY: But that's you all over —

JASON: I'm losing my mind.

JIMMY: Eternally drowning in Judeo-Christian guilt.

JASON: Truly losing my mind.

JIMMY: It's not worth it.

JASON: What?

JIMMY: Kiss me.

JASON: Kiss you? Kiss you? For Christ's sake, I can't even *watch* people kiss anymore.

JIMMY: Jas —

JASON: No — No — I see people somewhere. Anywhere. In a movie theater or somewhere. Couples kissing. Soft, tender kisses. It makes me sick. Watching them. Sick.

(Jimmy moves toward him.)

JIMMY: It doesn't have to be like —

JASON: No. No. Don't you remember? Don't you? How can you — . . . When we would make love — and you would cry when I came because you said at that moment I would get the most beautiful look of pain on my face. And you were right. It hurt. It hurt to be inside you. To feel that much. To look at your face and watch someone trust that much. We had that. And look what I did to you. If I could do that to you. To *you*. What's to stop me from doing it to someone else?

JIMMY: What did you do that was so horrible?

JASON: Nothing! I did nothing! That's worth like twenty years in purgatory.

JIMMY: More like twenty-five I think.

JASON: What?

JIMMY: Well, there's a system you know.

JASON: Really? . . . Oh my God.

JIMMY: Jas —

JASON: Oh my God!

JIMMY: Jason, can you just laugh a little?

JASON: I am, like, doomed.

JIMMY: Jesus Jas, you went to all that trouble to save yourself, and you're walking around as if you were dead.

JASON: Sometimes I wish I were. I'm so scared. Things used to be beautiful. Certain things were always supposed to remain beautiful.

JIMMY: Come here.

JASON: No.

JIMMY: Let's roll around on the grass. Let's get so dizzy that we see the sky fall and the trees uproot.

JASON: No.

JIMMY: Let's stare up into the sun and go blind so that all we'll be left with is Smell and Taste and Touch.

JASON: Don't do this —

JIMMY: Just drench ourselves with dirt and leaves and mud and —

JASON: Why are you doing this to me?!

JIMMY: It's hard Jas. It's hard to decide that life is better. And it is. It is better. To share. With someone. With some *one*. It's better than what you've been — . . . And to kiss? Antony and Cleopatra changed the world with a kiss. Their kiss changed the maps of the earth. Altered history . . . Come on. A kiss.

(They kiss.)

JUVENILIA
Wendy MacLeod

Comic
Henry and Brodie, twenty to twenty-two

> *Henry and Brodie are college students at an elite liberal arts college.*
> *Brodie is a "party animal"; Henry is more of a "nice guy." Brodie*
> *has come over to Henry's dorm room to hang out and talk about*
> *women. Henry would rather finish his routine on his exercycle.*
> *Henry's dorm room. Friday night. He is pedaling madly on an ex-*
> *ercise bike. A radio is on: the sound of some game. An iguana is in*
> *a glass aquarium. Brodie taps on the glass, the way that people seem*
> *compelled to do. Beside the aquarium, there is an open laptop.*

BRODIE: Nelly, Nelly, Nelly, did you miss me . . . ? Nelly is the only woman
that really, and I mean, truly, loves me.

HENRY: Iguanas don't love.

BRODIE: That is such bullshit. *(Pointing to Nelly.)* Look! I got the tongue.

HENRY: It's her dinner time.

BRODIE: Can I feed her?

HENRY: The crickets are on the shelf.

BRODIE: Live crickets?

HENRY: She only eats them if they're alive.

BRODIE: *(To Nelly.)* Nelly. You're an animal. *(To Henry.)* "Listen to Mister
Cricket singing his merry song." What's that from?

HENRY: I don't know.

BRODIE: Listen to Mister Cricket singing his merry song. Listen to Mister Cricket singing his merry song . . .

HENRY: Stop it.

> *(Brodie tries to get a single cricket out of a jar full of crickets.)*

BRODIE: That is a classic line from a classic something . . .

HENRY: You pick them up by the leg.

> *(Brodie puts the lid back on the jar.)*

BRODIE: I can't do it. On account of Mister Cricket's merry song. How can you hear yourself think?

(Brodie turns off the radio.)

HENRY: I don't have to think. I'm exercising.

BRODIE: Why don't you ride a real bike?

HENRY: Then I'd have to go somewhere.

BRODIE: So?

HENRY: This way I can stay here.

BRODIE: How long you got?

HENRY: Five more minutes.

BRODIE: *(Looking at the bike's controls.) Zero* incline. You pussy!

HENRY: I'm working up to it.

BRODIE: To what? The *prairie?*

HENRY: I thought you had a date tonight.

BRODIE: People don't date. Who do you know that dates? It's some 1950s *Happy Days* fantasy. People are fucking or they're not fucking. Think about it. What "dating" implies is that women are seeing more than one guy, right? To the Harvest dance with Roger on Friday night, to the malt shop with Ned Nickerson Saturday night, and a what, a "study date" with George on Sunday afternoon. So in the days when that ended with a kiss at the door, that's cool, but now what? She's boning three different guys? That's skanky.

HENRY: What happened with Meredith?

BRODIE: I used the word *tit* in conversation.

HENRY: You did what?

BRODIE: *(Defensively.)* I wasn't referring to *her* tits!

HENRY: Well whose tits were you referring to?

BRODIE: I simply said that a certain actress/singer had nice tits.

HENRY: Who?

BRODIE: It's not important.

HENRY: You don't praise another woman's body. Jesus. Everybody knows that.

BRODIE: That wasn't the issue.

HENRY: Believe me that was the issue . . .

BRODIE: The issue was the use of the word *tit.*

HENRY: So she broke up with you?

BRODIE: Why not call a spade a spade and a tit a tit?

HENRY: You should call them breasts.

BRODIE: Why?

HENRY: Because that's what they are.

BRODIE: Breasts. That's hard to say. It's like saying the word *scrotum*.

HENRY: No it isn't. *Scrotum* is a word that sounds like an insult. "What a scrotum!"

BRODIE: "What a breast!"

HENRY: See? It's different. *Breast* is a pretty word.

BRODIE: I don't know, it's got too many *esses*. *(Testing the word.)* "Breasts." I feel like I have a harelip. *(Testing again.)* Britney Spears has nice "breasts."

HENRY: They're totally fake!

BRODIE: So is Polar Fleece but it's warm and soft.

HENRY: Britney's breasts may look great but they feel like shit!

BRODIE: Oh you know that.

HENRY: I've *heard* that.

BRODIE: You've spoken to someone who felt up Britney Spears.

HENRY: No. To someone whose girlfriend had her tits enlarged.

BRODIE: *(Pouncing on the word* tits.*)* Tits! Tits!

HENRY: You can say the word when there's not a woman in the room.

BRODIE: *(Solemnly.)* You . . . hypocrite.

HENRY: Why is that hypocritical?

BRODIE: If it's not alright to say it then it's never alright to say it. Is it alright to use the word *nigger* when your black friends aren't around?

HENRY: You're the one who called a spade a spade!

BRODIE: So?

HENRY: That's a derogatory term for African Americans!

BRODIE: That's not what it means!

HENRY: Well what else could it mean?

BRODIE: The card. The . . . suit. Hearts, clubs, diamonds, spades.

HENRY: Still, you shouldn't say "tit" around Meredith.

BRODIE: Go ahead. Take her side. I knew you would . . .

HENRY: Why?

BRODIE: Because you want to fuck her. Your pupils dilate when she comes into the room.

HENRY: Why are you looking at my pupils?

BRODIE: I'm onto you my friend. You're going to play nice guy to my asshole for as long as it takes for her to see that you're the one who really loves and respects her.

HENRY: *(Struggling for rebuttal.)* Not!

BRODIE: Snappy comeback. How much longer?

HENRY: *(Looking at his gauge.)* Two thirty-six.

BRODIE: Look at you. You're sweating like a stuck pig.

HENRY: It's fucking hot in here.

BRODIE: What are you complaining about? You're like going *downhill.*

HENRY: Don't you ever have homework?

BRODIE: We have something more important to do, my friend.

HENRY: No.

BRODIE: Come on . . .

HENRY: I'm not doing it.

BRODIE: You did it before.

HENRY: In a weak moment . . .

BRODIE: I'll click on the 3-way!

HENRY: Do it in your own room.

BRODIE: My computer's fucked up.

HENRY: My next-door neighbor uses that computer.

BRODIE: Is this the black girl?

HENRY: Yes.

BRODIE: The hot one?

> *(Henry nods.)*

BRODIE: Is that like a thing of yours? Black girls?

HENRY: She's just . . . nice and I don't want her to see I've been visiting porn sites.

BRODIE: We'll cover our asses with a multitude of Encyclopedia Britannica hits.

HENRY: Why are you perving up to a screen when you could be out with a real woman?

BRODIE: Real women don't do what you tell them.

HENRY: You're afraid of a real woman . . .

BRODIE: And you're afraid of a bike with two wheels!

HENRY: This is more convenient!

BRODIE: Exactly!

HENRY: The picture quality is awful. The pictures take like forever to download. And the lighting is dreadful.

BRODIE: *(English accent.)* Good evening, it's Alistair Cooke with Masturbate Theater. Come on, I want to see me lady Tiffany.

(Brodie sits at the computer and starts clicking on porn sites.)

HENRY: Whose real name is probably Margaret.

BRODIE: Why do you have to ruin it for me?

HENRY: So where's Meredith?

BRODIE: I don't know. Am I my girlfriend's keeper?

HENRY: Is she still your girlfriend?

BRODIE: If she isn't, there's a lengthy roster of women willing to take her place.

HENRY: Does it matter to you whether it's Meredith?

BRODIE: It matters to me too fucking much actually but I can't be censoring my vocabulary, my sexual impulses, my very self.

HENRY: So how is the sweetheart of Sigma Phi?

BRODIE: Uggh. She seems to be under the impression that we're "dating."

HENRY: I wonder where she got that idea . . .

BRODIE: It was a random hookup. She knows I've got a girlfriend.

HENRY: And yet sometimes you behave as if you don't.

BRODIE: When the cat's away . . .

HENRY: The cat was visiting her *sick mother* . . .

BRODIE: I know I did a bad thing. Mea culpa, it's over . . .

HENRY: Her *dying* mother . . .

BRODIE: I know! *Jesus. (To the computer screen.) Hello* Tiffany of the lengthy nipples.

HENRY: Keep your voice down.

BRODIE: Tiffany looks a little young, don't you think?

HENRY: Yes. Which is one of the many reasons that site is creepy.

BRODIE: Tell me Henry, do you even like women?

HENRY: Oh that is getting so tired . . .

BRODIE: Well it's not like you're on a *team* . . .

HENRY: I am cycling!

BRODIE: *(With a lisp.)* "I am cycling!" How gay is that?

HENRY: Just because I don't like porn doesn't mean I'm not into women!

BRODIE: No, just because you're not into beautiful women with big breasts doesn't mean . . .

HENRY: I like beautiful women, God, I love beautiful women, I just, frankly I don't see the point of getting myself any hornier than I am already! I mean, at the moment, there is no chance that I'm going to be able to act on the multitude of urges that I have already so why exacerbate them by having some cartoon offer to give me a blow job!

BRODIE: They're not cartoons. They're real women.

HENRY: Shot on digital in some warehouse in Van Nuys.

BRODIE: Does that make them any less real?

HENRY: They're like prostitutes, Brodie. They don't actually want you.

BRODIE: Tiffany wants me bad.

HENRY: She's like filing her nails mentally. The entire sex industry should be shut down. It's like the death of love.

BRODIE: We have got to get you laid. This dearth of snatch is turning you into Oliver Cromwell.

HENRY: Tell me about Oliver Cromwell, Brodie . . .

BRODIE: I know about Puritans!

HENRY: You failed that class.

BRODIE: You know what you need?

HENRY: Shut up.

BRODIE: You're alone in a room with an iguana, man. That's sick.

HENRY: You're the one who's going on about her tongue!

BRODIE: What Nelly and I have is pure. . . .

OUR LADY OF 121ST STREET

Stephen Adly Guirgis

Comic

Rooftop, thirties; Father Lux, any age

> *Rooftop is a popular Los Angeles DJ. He has returned to New York*
> *for the funeral of a nun who was a much-beloved teacher at a*
> *Catholic school. The play takes place mostly in a funeral home. The*
> *body of Sister Rose has inexplicably disappeared. Various mourners,*
> *including Rooftop, are waiting for the police to solve the mystery of*
> *the missing body. While he waits, Rooftop decides to confess his many*
> *transgressions to a priest at a nearby church.*

ROOFTOP: Bless me Father for I have sinned . . . *(Pause.)* . . . a lot, know
what I'm sayin'? . . . Yes sir . . . Um . . . Are you, Are you there, Father? . . .

FATHER LUX: Yes.

ROOFTOP: Alright, juss checkin' . . . That you, Father Martin?

FATHER LUX: Uh, no.

ROOFTOP: Father Cunningham?

FATHER LUX: No.

ROOFTOP: Oh . . . Where Father Cunningham at?

FATHER LUX: Excuse me?

ROOFTOP: I say, where Father Cunningham at?

FATHER LUX: Father Cunningham?

ROOFTOP: Yeah.

FATHER LUX: He's — no longer with us.

ROOFTOP: Father C., you talkin' 'bout?

FATHER LUX: Yes.

ROOFTOP: "No longer with us," huh?

FATHER LUX: Yes.

ROOFTOP: Father C.?

FATHER LUX: Correct.

ROOFTOP: Dag . . . He didn't do something "bad," did he?

FATHER LUX: He's dead.

ROOFTOP: Dead?!

FATHER LUX: With God, yes.

ROOFTOP: Well, pardon me, but — why didn't you just say that then?

FATHER LUX: What?

ROOFTOP: I'm sayin', if the man's dead, juss say he dead.

FATHER LUX: I did.

ROOFTOP: Nah, you said "no longer with us" — like, like a "scandal" or
   something.

FATHER LUX: Are you here to make confession, sir?

ROOFTOP: Yes I am, but Father C. was a close, personal friend of mine,
   and I can't really say I appreciate —

FATHER LUX: Father Cunningham has been dead for fifteen years, sir, OK?!
   (Pause.)

ROOFTOP: Oh . . . OK . . . Sorry . . .

FATHER LUX: . . . So, how long since your last confession?

ROOFTOP: My last confession?

FATHER LUX: Yes.

ROOFTOP: The last one?

FATHER LUX: Yes.

ROOFTOP: You mean in a church?

FATHER LUX: In a church. Yes.

ROOFTOP: Right. Well . . . last one been . . . well . . . well, it's been . . .
   Know what I'm sayin'? It's been been. Definitely been been.

FATHER LUX: OK.

ROOFTOP: Put it like this: my first confession? That was the last time
   checkin' in with y'all, so, yeah, been a while . . . been . . . well —

FATHER LUX: Got it. Proceed.

ROOFTOP: 'Cuz I mean, ya know, my moms raised me right, went to school
   right upstairs, listened ta the nuns, Sister Rose and all, still . . . Shit!
   Is Father C. really dead?

FATHER LUX: What?

ROOFTOP: 'Cuz I was hopin' ta get Father C.

FATHER LUX: Sir —

ROOFTOP: Guess everybody got ta go, right?

FATHER LUX: Yes.

ROOFTOP: Still, how's a man gonna up and die with no warning?

FATHER LUX: Sir —

ROOFTOP: Send a telegram, sumpthin': "Might die soon. FYI."

FATHER LUX: Perhaps you ought to collect yourself and come back later.

ROOFTOP: Hey Father, did you know that Father C. one time got hit by a Mack truck but he was OK?

FATHER LUX: Sir —

ROOFTOP: See, us kids, we was playin' Booties Up on the wall across from here, but we was all standin' in the street like fools do, and —

FATHER LUX: Stop.

ROOFTOP: What, I can't relate a little anecdote?

FATHER LUX: What you can do, sir, is confess.

ROOFTOP: Confess, huh?

FATHER LUX: Confess your sins. Yes.

ROOFTOP: Dag, you all business, ain'tcha, Father?

FATHER LUX: Sir —

ROOFTOP: No prelude nuthin' — just spit it out.

FATHER LUX: — Sir —

ROOFTOP: — "Early birds eat apples and worms," I gotcha — got no argument wit' that.

FATHER LUX: OK then.

ROOFTOP: You got a forthright nature, Father — no nonsense — I respect that in a man.

FATHER LUX: Oh. Well —

ROOFTOP: Still, even Hank Aaron hit a few off the practice tee before he stepped up to the rock — gotta marinate before ya grill, right?

FATHER LUX: This is not a "cookout," sir.

ROOFTOP: No, it's not —

FATHER LUX: No charcoal, no anecdotes, no franks and beans —

ROOFTOP: — True dat —

FATHER LUX: This is, in fact, a confessional, sir. A confessional — not a "conversational" — do you understand that distinction?

ROOFTOP: I'll keep it moving.

FATHER LUX: Thank you.

ROOFTOP: OK . . . right: So . . . So, yeah — I mean, whaddyacallit? The inter Venal Sins?

FATHER LUX: Venal.

ROOFTOP: What?

FATHER LUX: Venal.

ROOFTOP: Venal yeah — mucho venal. Venal Sins, dass daily, daily occurrence. Prolly racked up a dozen since I walked up in here . . . And, uh, Mortal Sins? Mortal Sins, Father? I mean, "pick a Commandment, any Commandment," know what I'm sayin'?

FATHER LUX: How 'bout you pick one?

ROOFTOP: Oh . . . OK . . . uh . . . Dag, Father, I'm juss, I'm juss a bad man, Father. Lyin', cheatin', stealin', and humpin' — Dag. Freebasing . . . See, I'm the kind of guy . . . one time I . . . well, there was this girl once . . . say Father, I can't smoke in here, right?

OUR LADY OF
121ST STREET
Stephen Adly Guirgis

Comic
Pinky and Edwin, twenties to thirties

> *Pinky and Edwin have come to a funeral home to mourn the death*
> *of a nun who was their much-beloved teacher in Catholic school.*
> *Sister Rose's body has mysteriously disappeared, though, and Pinky*
> *and Edwin are whiling away the time while they wait for the po-*
> *lice to solve the mystery of the missing body. They are brothers.*

EDWIN: *(To himself.)* "Sister Rose Marie was a very special person. I, per-
sonally, had her for homeroom for first grade, and for second grade,
and then for second grade again, and then for second grade one more
time, which is why I respected (No, not respected), which is why, even
though she beat my ass wit'a shilaylee. (Nah, dat ain't right.)"

PINKY: Edwin —

EDWIN: "We always loved her, even when we didn't" —

PINKY: Edwin —

EDWIN: Shut up, Pinky, I'm tryin' ta put my thoughts in place —

PINKY: Oh . . . OK.

EDWIN: Put that cigarette out, you can't smoke in here.

PINKY: Sorry —

EDWIN: Wait. Gimme a drag first . . . "We loved her 'cuz" —

PINKY: You want a fresh one?

EDWIN: Nah . . . Yeah. Whatchu smokin'?

PINKY: Kool Breeze.

EDWIN: Kool Breeze? What the fuck kinda brand is dat?

PINKY: Two dollar eighty-five.

EDWIN: Fuck dat . . . You got any chocolate?

PINKY: I could get some.

EDWIN: You could get me two packs a Yodels?

PINKY: You wanna juss split a box?

EDWIN: Nah . . . Yeah. You need money?

PINKY: Maybe juss like four dollars.

EDWIN: In other words, you need money.

PINKY: I guess.

EDWIN: So juss say dat then.

PINKY: I didn't wanna upset your concentration.

EDWIN: Well, it's upset.

PINKY: Sorry.

EDWIN: Not on account a you, Pink, alright?

PINKY: . . . OK.

EDWIN: Are you sayin' "OK" like you believe me? Or, are you juss sayin, "OK"?

PINKY: Like I believe you.

EDWIN: Are you sure? I don' wanna see you start cryin', 'cuz, I juss couldn't handle that right now.

PINKY: I ain't gonna cry.

EDWIN: I mean, if you feel like cryin', cry. 'Cuz, I don' wanna stifle your feelin's or nuthin' —

PINKY: I ain't stifled.

EDWIN: It's juss, I need you strong over here.

PINKY: I'm strong . . . Wanna feel my muscle?

EDWIN: Look, here's a twenty-dollar bill, OK? Wit' the Yodels? Get a quart of milk.

PINKY: OK.

EDWIN: Regular, not skim or some shit. The red one.

PINKY: I know.

EDWIN: And check the date. On the Yodels too. Grab the milk from the back.

PINKY: I got three girlfriends, Edwin.

EDWIN: That's great. Bring me the change.

PINKY: They're all pretty . . . except one.

EDWIN: I gotta get back to this, Pinky.

PINKY: OK . . . You're gonna make a great Analogy, Edwin.

EDWIN: Eulogy, Pinky. Not analogy. Eulogy.

PINKY: I'm gonna tell her all about it when I get home.

EDWIN: Great . . . tell who?

PINKY: Sister Rose.

EDWIN: Pinky . . . Bro . . . Sister Rose is dead, you know dat right?

PINKY: I know.

EDWIN: Dead, like, dead.

PINKY: I know.

EDWIN: Like Mom and Dad, right?

PINKY: Yeah . . . And the Super. Mr. Regal.

EDWIN: Yeah . . . Dead like them, right?

PINKY: In Heaven.

EDWIN: Dass right . . .

PINKY: Eatin' cheeseburgers.

EDWIN: Watchin' Pay-Per-View for free with the Blessed Mother and Saint Anthony, and Mom and Dad.

PINKY: And Mr. Regal.

EDWIN: Yes . . . Now, Pinky: When Balthazar's partner came in here and asked us those questions, you answered the truth, right?

PINKY: Whaddya mean?

EDWIN: I mean, if I were to go up to our apartment right now, I wouldn't find anyone that ain't supposed to be there, right?

PINKY: . . . You mean like Mrs. McNulty's cat?

EDWIN: Never mind. Go get the Yodels now.

PINKY: I wantcha to meet my girlfriends.

EDWIN: I'm lookin' forward to it . . . Yodels. Go. *(Pause.)*

PINKY: I didn't mean to upset your concentration, Edwin.

EDWIN: I know that Pinky.

PINKY: I think . . . can I say something, Edwin?

EDWIN: Is it sumpthin' short?

PINKY: Pretty short.

EDWIN: So say it then.

PINKY: Actually, it's two things.

EDWIN: I didn't agree to hearing two things, Pinky.

PINKY: I'll make it quick.

EDWIN: Juss fuckin' say it already.

PINKY: OK: Do you think that girl Norca is gonna be here today and can I have a hug please?

EDWIN: How many hugs have I given you today?

PINKY: Only like six.

EDWIN: So go get the Yodels and milk, bring me the change, and I'll give you another hug. How's that?

PINKY: A long hug?

EDWIN: Would you just get the fuckin' Yodels already?!

PINKY: Oh. OK . . . What about Norca?

EDWIN: Forget about Norca, she don't like you. Eat some Yodels and forget about that shit.

PINKY: I really would feel better if you —

EDWIN: Oh fuckin' Jesus fuckin' Christ Pinky! Come over here!

(Pinky crosses to Edwin. They hug.)

THE REEVES TALE
Don Nigro

Dramatic
John, twenty-seven; Alen, twenty-seven

> *In rural east Ohio in 1972 John and Alen, college grads who are*
> *now drifters, are hired hands at the Pendragon house, a huge old*
> *falling-apart mansion, where they work for Sim Reeves, who rents*
> *the place to farm the land. John and Alen live in very cramped quar-*
> *ters in a couple of rooms of the house with Sim, who's a vulgar, piglike*
> *man, his intelligent and attractive, sad wife Abby, Abby's annoying*
> *grandfather Pap, and Abby and Sim's beautiful sixteen-year-old*
> *daughter Molkin. Alen has just been teasing Abby and John about*
> *their attraction to one another, and Abby has left the room, upset.*

JOHN: Leave her alone.

ALEN: Don't get touchy. I'm just teasing her. She's got no sense of humor, is all. You like that woman, do you?

JOHN: Let's get to work.

ALEN: Better than the girl?

JOHN: One's too young and the other one's married.

ALEN: So who'd that ever stop?

JOHN: You keep bothering her, it might just give him the excuse he's been looking for to run us off without paying us. You better watch Sim. He's not exactly playing with a full deck, and with all the guns and knives around here, I don't think I'd mess with him.

ALEN: I'm gonna have that girl tonight, Johnny.

JOHN: No you're not.

ALEN: While he's sleeping. I'm gonna do it right under his nose. Hell, I damn near had her in the barn the other day. She was teasin' me, but he watches her like a hawk. I had to stop HER when old Sim came yelling after her round the back of the house. She had her shirt open and her pants half off, and her hand on my little friend Dicky. If Sim wasn't so damned stupid he'd have caught us half a dozen times. She wants it bad, John. She's just scared he'll wring her neck. There ain't no harm in it if she wants it and says so and damn near crawls all over me every time she gets the chance. I ain't gonna force her or nothing. Christ, what do you take me for?

JOHN: Alen, the man is a gorilla.

ALEN: He'll be drunker than a skunk tonight, and when he gets drunk he sleeps like a rock, and he don't half know what's going on if he wakes up anyway.

JOHN: What about Abby?

ALEN: That's your job.

JOHN: Oh, no. Just leave me out of it.

ALEN: Come on, John. You owe me.

JOHN: For what?

ALEN: I'm your friend.

JOHN: I keep forgetting.

ALEN: Didn't I fix you up with Susie Leakey?

JOHN: You were trying to get rid of her.

ALEN: What about Ramona Zorkin?

JOHN: I never slept with Ramona Zorkin.

ALEN: What, are you crazy? Why the hell not?

JOHN: Ramona Zorkin had the clap.

ALEN: How do you know?

JOHN: She told me.

ALEN: Well, how was I supposed to know that?

JOHN: You gave it to her.

ALEN: It was her birthday.

JOHN: I don't want to get involved in this, all right?

ALEN: You're talkin to the guy who babysat your damned German Shepherd all the time you was in the service.

JOHN: The dog died.

ALEN: He missed you. He committed suicide. Who was it got the shit beat out of him when them rednecks jumped you in the bar that time? Huh? I could have pretended I didn't know you, John. Christ, I lost a tooth in that. Who drove you to El Paso to see that girl with the long hair? Who painted half your apartment? Who went to your mother's funeral with you? Who slept in the dorm lobby when you had Diane Roselli there for the weekend?

JOHN: What do you want me to do?

ALEN: I got it all planned, like a military operation, just like the Bay of Pigs or something. OK, bad example. Look, we got three beds here, right? Just like the three bears. Now, before Sim hired us, they slept Sim and Abby in the one over on the end, right?

JOHN: I guess so. Who cares?

ALEN: They're disoriented, John, because to make room for us, we got Molkin's old bed on the other end, which you and me share, and she's in the near bed with Abby, and Sim's in the middle with Pap. So once Sim gets to snoring good, and Molkin goes to sleep, what does Abby do? She goes out in the kitchen and smokes a cigarette. Every night. Just like clockwork. So when she goes out for her smoke, you follow her out there and keep her busy for half an hour or so, talk to her or something. Hell, screw her on the table if she'll let you, that asshole Sim is driving her nuts. She could probably use a little something to take her mind off her life. You know, you two being so sensitive and all.

JOHN: I run interference with the mother while you deflower the daughter.

ALEN: John, that girl ain't been a flower since she was fourteen. She knows what she's doing, believe me. And Abby don't care. What does she care? Come on, take a chance. You might get lucky. This is America, here. This is like the spirit of free enterprise at work, John. You know what I mean? John? Please?

ROUNDING THIRD
Richard Dresser

Comic
Michael and Don, thirties to forties

> *Michael and Don are Little League baseball coaches. Don's the Head*
> *Coach; Michael's the Assistant Coach, and something of a neophyte*
> *on the job. He has volunteered because his son, a total clutz, has come*
> *out for the team. Don and Michael are having an argument about*
> *managerial strategy.*

DON: We have lost our best player. I feel responsible that it is my kid putting
　　on makeup and prancing about in tights instead of whiffing guys with
　　his fastball. I lie awake nights thinking about how we can make up
　　for that terrible gaping hole in our lineup. I owe this to the kids.

MICHAEL: Let them play, Don. Just let them play. It's OK.

DON: That's very impressive strategy. "Just let them play." Did you come
　　up with that while you were the only car stuck in traffic?

MICHAEL: Let me ask you something. What do you think the Commis-
　　sioner would have to say about this?

DON: Our Commissioner was convicted of transporting cigarettes over state
　　lines for the purpose of illegal sales. So I can't imagine my Little League
　　game strategy will put his panties in a twirl. Now let me ask you some-
　　thing about dedication and commitment. Do you ever think about
　　the team when you aren't actually here?

MICHAEL: Yes, I do.

DON: How much?

MICHAEL: A lot.

DON: Waking hours, what percentage?

MICHAEL: What percentage of my waking hours do I spend thinking about
　　the team?

DON: I would say with me it's 55 percent. Easy. Then I think about money maybe 25 percent of the time. And the rest is all sex and revenge fantasies. You honestly don't know your percentages?

MICHAEL: I haven't stopped to figure it out, Don.

DON: Gee, a bright, successful big shot like you, and you never even stopped to think about what you think about? And then you come here to the field where I have coached my heart out for the last seven years and stab me in the back in front of my team. Ever read the rule book, Michael?

MICHAEL: No.

DON: Course not. Because it might get in the way of your candy-ass opinions. Well, you should know that my new strategy is fully sanctioned by the official Little League rule book. Injured runners may be replaced.

MICHAEL: But they're not really injured. They're just *acting* injured.

DON: *Acting?* Was that a shot at Jimmy?

MICHAEL: No, it was a shot at you. For getting so carried away with winning you'd teach these kids to cheat.

DON: Fact: You serve here at my discretion. If I say the word you're an ex-Assistant Coach and I am so close to saying the word I can taste it.

MICHAEL: You know I'm right.

DON: I know there's no place for you in baseball. A man who doesn't care if he wins, who has nothing to teach his son except the finer points of being a loser.

MICHAEL: Don't call me a loser. And don't drag my son into this.

DON: Fine. Then don't you mention Jimmy.

MICHAEL: I won't.

DON: Because Jimmy is the best player on the team.

MICHAEL: Except he isn't on the team.

DON: I'm warning you, Michael. You've been no help to me this season. I've had to do everything, schedules, snacks, fungoes.

MICHAEL: You're still angry I broke the window of your van.

DON: I wasn't talking about that.

MICHAEL: I offered to pay and you wouldn't let me. You wanted to hold it over me.

DON: Let's be honest here, Michael. We both know why you kept offering to pay.

MICHAEL: Because I felt responsible.

DON: You couldn't cut it as coach so you had to fling your money in my face. You and your big-shot company.

MICHAEL: What are you talking about?

DON: Your company, Michael, couldn't wait to tell me you had your own company —

MICHAEL: It isn't my company.

DON: Oh, really? Then we can add "liar" to your rap sheet. I know for a fact you shot off your mouth about "my company" with the "government contracts."

MICHAEL: I meant the company where I work. My company. "My company has offices in Japan . . ."

DON: I frankly don't care where the hell your company has offices, Michael —

MICHAEL: I'm giving an example of how I meant it was just a company I work for. Not *my* company.

DON: OK, deeply misleading, but I accept that. The point is, you wanted to pay for my windshield to show you were the one with the high-dollar job while I'm just a jerk with a van —

MICHAEL: Don, again, you're so deeply wrong.

DON: I have stood right here countless times with my clipboard while you take phone calls that you think are more important than the kids.

MICHAEL: I take those calls from my boss. Roger. A twenty-four-year-old guy who likes to order me around. I used to have an OK job but I got busted down to being Roger's assistant because I missed so much work.

DON: Tardy? Stuck in unbelievable traffic?

MICHAEL: I missed a lot of work when my wife was sick.

DON: Boy, you just can't wait to play that trump card, can you?

MICHAEL: And I was late today because I had to make sure Roger's new office furniture arrived. I don't think that's what a big shot would be doing.

DON: It wouldn't be a problem. All you had to do is call.

MICHAEL: I did call.

DON: You didn't talk to me.

MICHAEL: I talked to Linda. Your wife.

DON: Linda, my wife? Nice try. Linda was at a School Board meeting that went late. She didn't even get home till eleven-thirty.

MICHAEL: I called at 7:30.

DON: Did you tell her you'd be late for practice?

MICHAEL: She said she was on the other line and she'd get back to me.

DON: Yeah? And did she?

MICHAEL: What happened was she got back on my line but she must have thought she was still on the other line.

DON: Why do you think that?

MICHAEL: She said, "I'll meet you at the usual place."

DON: Who was she talking to?

MICHAEL: Beats me. I was on my line, she was on hers.

DON: She must have said a name.

MICHAEL: Nope.

DON: You're a terrible liar.

MICHAEL: That's not true. My wife used to think I was a pretty darn good liar.

DON: So you're lying?

MICHAEL: No, she really thought I was a good liar.

DON: Are you lying about this person my wife said she'd meet?

MICHAEL: That part is all true.

DON: OK. So tell me the name she used.

MICHAEL: Think about it, Don, she wouldn't necessarily use a name —

DON: But she *did* use a name, didn't she?

> *(Beat.)*

> Give me the name, Michael. Or there's going to be some serious trouble here at the George "Bucky" Philips Community Park.

MICHAEL: Look, the kids are coming back.

DON: *(Yells to team.)* Hey! Take another lap! *(Beat.)* Because conditioning is important for the play-offs! You want to be champions?

> *(Don turns back to Michael, who's put on a catcher's mask.)*

DON: *(Continuing.)* What the hell are you doing, Michael?

MICHAEL: Are we going to have a fistfight?

DON: Of course not, pal. Take off the mask.

> *(Michael takes off the mask.)*

DON: *(Continuing.)* And tell me what Linda said.

MICHAEL: What if I don't tell you?

DON: *(Grabs a bat.)* I'll kill you. But rest assured, we won't fight.
  (Don puts Michael in a choke hold.)

MICHAEL: Stop, please! You said we wouldn't fight!

DON: Don't fight back; then we won't be fighting. *(Holds tighter, choking him.)* The one thing you need to know is, I will do this. I will choke the life right out of you. What did she say?

MICHAEL: *(Mumbled.)*

DON: Huh?

MICHAEL: *(Mumbled.)*

DON: What?

MICHAEL: She said . . . I'll meet you at the usual place, Tee-Bee.

DON: Tee-Bee?

MICHAEL: I don't know. It sounded like that.

DON: Tee-Bee. Tony Barone. *(Lets Michael go.)* I never wanted to get Call Waiting.

MICHAEL: I agree. People will always call back if it's important. *(Beat.)* I'm sure there's an explanation.

DON: Of course there is. A damn good explanation.

MICHAEL: There you go! *(Beat.)* What do you think it is?

DON: Either they were planning a surprise party for me, or my wife's banging my best friend.

MICHAEL: Boy, wouldn't it be great if it was a surprise party? *(Beat.)* Don?

DON: Before you talk, remember you're strictly prohibited from cheering me up. Still want to talk?

MICHAEL: No.

DON: Goddamn it. *(Re: Clipboard.)* How would you like to have a look at the clipboard?

MICHAEL: You mean it? I can't believe you're actually letting me look at the clipboard.

DON: Stats on each kid, my analysis of their progress, game by game. You'll find general team philosophy. Bullet points of pregame speeches, amusing and inspirational anecdotes. School or family pressures we should be aware of.

MICHAEL: What's going on, Don?

DON: I think it's time to drop the "Assistant" from your job description.

Scenes for
Two Women

ENCHANTED APRIL
Matthew Barber

Dramatic
Lotty, thirty; Rose, thirty-eight

>   *Lotty and Rose are both British housewives, to varying degrees un-*
>   *satisfied with their lives. In this, the opening scene of the play, they*
>   *meet for the first time and discuss whether they should go off on their*
>   *own for a holiday in Italy — without their husbands. Pretty dar-*
>   *ing for 1922!*

>   *Darkness. Half-light rises on two tables, four chairs, a coat rack with*
>   *coats and umbrellas. Rose Arnott sits at one table. Lotty Wilton stands*
>   *at the other, looking off. Thunder, followed by the sound of steady*
>   *rain. Lights up in a London ladies' club, 1922. "The Great War"*
>   *is over by four years, and with it the lives of one million British sol-*
>   *diers. Rose reads a copy of the London* Times. *Lotty gazes out of a*
>   *large window. Both are dressed heavily in dark colors, hair up, with*
>   *hats on or nearby. Lotty's appearance suggests uncertainty. Rose is spare*
>   *to the point of severity. Lotty speaks to us. Her essence is of deep sad-*
>   *ness and withering valiance, from which genuine hope spontaneously*
>   *and regularly bursts forth, leaving her endlessly off-balance.*

LOTTY: I was once told the story of a man who, while surveying the grounds
of his home, dug his walking stick into the earth, as a reminder of
where he wished to one day have an acacia tree. One he could watch
from his veranda, and lie under with his wife on warm summer af-
ternoons, cooled in the shadow of its white flowers, and blanketed
in their sweet scent. But when planting season came 'round and he
returned with a spade and an acacia sapling, the man was vexed. The
stick he had left had taken root and begun to grow. It was nearly as
tall as himself now, in fact, with young, awkward branches and small
clusters of frail new leaves. This, on the very spot that was to be his
acacia. The man buried his spade into the ground to unearth the

strange thing . . . but stopped. For among the leaves, underneath, he spied a small blossom. It was acacia. *(Smiles.)* "Enchantment," some would say. Or "providence," perhaps. I suppose the only real certainty is that the fellow had lost a perfectly good walking stick. If that's the part you choose to see. The rest is open to opinion. *(Sighs, thinks.)* Were it only that some enchantment would step in for us all, to change what we have into what we wish for. To bridge the awkward gap between all of our many "befores" and "afters". Because, for every "after" found, a "before" must be lost. And loss is, by nature, an unbalancing thing. More unbalancing, however, is to discover your "before" gone without an "after" having taken its place. Leaving you merely to wait and to wonder if there is to be an "after" at all. Or if, perhaps, waiting and wondering are your "after" in themselves. *(Thinks.)* I wasn't expecting my "after" to begin that day at my ladies' club. I wasn't waiting for enchantment to show itself, or providence. I had merely been gazing out of the window, wondering if the rain was ever going to stop. And what my husband might like for dinner that night. And about the fact that the day before I had wondered the same things. And surely would the following day, and the day after that, and the day after. When I came upon the advertisement.

ROSE: *(Reading.)* "To those who appreciate wisteria and sunshine . . ."

LOTTY: A small advert, placed discreetly in the agony column of the *Times*.

ROSE: "Small castle on the Mediterranean, Northern Italy . . ."

LOTTY: Heaven!

ROSE: "To be let for the month of April. Cook, gardens, ocean view. Reply Box Eleven."

LOTTY: *(Beaming.)* The words washed over me, filling me suddenly with warmth and peacefulness, as if the advertisement were there especially for me, and was pleased I'd found it. "To those who appreciate wisteria and sunshine." That's me! *(Thunder. Thinks.)* But who am I to be reading about Italian castles, and Aprils on the Mediterranean? Who am I? *(Inspired.)* But then, why would I bother to read the newspaper at my ladies' club, when I surely would read my husband's copy tomorrow morning after housekeeping? And why would I come to my club at all on a Tuesday, when my regular city day is Wednesday? And certainly why would I notice the lady, that particular lady I see so often at church, and was thinking of only moments ago? Providence? Enchantment? *(She smiles excitedly. To Rose, with great enthusiasm.)* Are you reading about the castle and the wisteria?

ROSE: *(Invaded.)* I beg your pardon?

LOTTY: *(Breathlessly.)* The advertisement about the castle. It sounds so wonderful, doesn't it? Can you just imagine? Italy and sunshine and wisteria. And when I saw you . . . you, of all people . . . well, I couldn't help but think . . . well, I mean, all this rain . . . and, oh, the Mediterranean . . . imagine . . . and this not even being my city day . . . well, I . . . I . . . *(Flustered, suddenly painfully uncomfortable, realizing that her intensity has once again escaped.)* Oh, I am sorry. Here we've only just met and I must apologize already. My husband says that my mind is like a hummingbird. One seldom sees it land. I feel I know you. And yet we've never actually met. My husband and I see you in church in Hampstead.

ROSE: I see.

LOTTY: You are our "disappointed Madonna." I see you each Sunday, marshalling in the children from Sunday School, always so right on time for services, and with the schoolchildren so very well-behaved. And I once commented to my husband that you looked to me somewhat like a disappointed Madonna.

ROSE: *(Perplexed.)* I . . .

LOTTY: My husband had been speaking to me about finding satisfaction through doing one's job well. Saying something about that if one does one's job well, then one will *not* be depressed, but will instead be automatically bright and brisk with satisfaction. And, seeing you, I just felt that . . . well, that surely there is also the chance for a certain . . . disappointment.

ROSE: *(Patiently.)* Perhaps it would be best if we begin at the beginning. I am Mrs. Arnott. Rose.

LOTTY: Thank you. I am Lotty. Charlotte. Mrs. Wilton.

ROSE: Right, then.

LOTTY: I don't expect that conveys much to you, "Wilton." Sometimes it doesn't seem to convey anything to me, either. Such a small, sad name. I don't like names.

ROSE: Do you need some kind of advice, Mrs. Wilton?

LOTTY: Oh, no. It was just the advertisement. It sounded so wonderful, that's all.

ROSE: I'm sure it's only this gloomy weather that makes it so.

LOTTY: Then you were reading it?

ROSE: *(Caught.)* I . . . was.

LOTTY: *(Excited.)* I knew it! I saw it!

ROSE: Saw it?

LOTTY: The two of us. At the castle.

ROSE: Yourself and your husband.

LOTTY: Oh no, me and you!

ROSE: Mrs. Wilton!

LOTTY: Do you ever see things in a kind of a flash before they happen?

ROSE: Never.

LOTTY: Really? Well, when I saw you, I suddenly saw us both, you and me, on the shores of the Mediterranean. Surrounded by beauty. Beauty and blissful peace.

ROSE: Really, Mrs. Wilton. And our husbands? *(Lotty thinks.)*

LOTTY: I didn't see them. I've never seen Mr. Arnott. He is "with us," then?

ROSE: Oh, yes. Quite.

LOTTY: One never knows these days. So many war widows.

ROSE: Sad times.

LOTTY: Perhaps that's why we need something beautiful now. To remind us of the possibility. I did see us, Rose.

ROSE: Well, that is really most extraordinary, Mrs. Wilton.

LOTTY: Isn't it? Isn't it wonderful enough just to think about? April in Italy. And here it's February already. In two months we could be in it all.

ROSE: It's easy to think of such things, Mrs. Wilton. But it's no use wasting one's time thinking too long.

LOTTY: Oh, but it is! It's essential! And I really do believe, if one considers hard enough, things can happen!

ROSE: I'm not sure I believe that.

LOTTY: *(Becoming increasingly emotional.)* Oh, but you must! Even if it isn't true. I've been saving a nest egg, from my dress allowance. It's not much, but my husband himself encouraged me to save it for a rainy day. My husband speaks often of rainy days. My husband speaks often of many things. I could never have imagined spending it on a holiday, but if this isn't that rainy day, well . . .

ROSE: Money, I fear . . .

LOTTY: Oh, Rose. Close your eyes and think with all of your heart of getting away from Hampstead, from husbands, from this relentless rain, from everything. To heaven!

ROSE: You shouldn't say things like that, Mrs. Wilton.

LOTTY: But it would be heavenly!

ROSE: Heaven isn't somewhere else. It is here and now, within us. We are told that on the very highest authority. The kindred points of heaven and home. Heaven is in our home. *(Lotty thinks.)*

LOTTY: But it isn't.

ROSE: But it is. It is there, if we choose, if we make it.

LOTTY: *(Upset, near tears.)* I do choose, and I do make it. And it isn't. I've done nothing but what was expected of me all of my life, and thought that was goodness. I thought I would be . . . well . . . rewarded in some way, I suppose. That's selfish, I know. But it was what I was told. One prepares, is good, and is rewarded. I didn't know how quickly things change. That one must keep an eye on what one is preparing for, in case it no longer even exists. Someone forgot to tell me that. Where everyone is racing to, I don't know. I only know that I've been left behind. No. Now I'm convinced that there are blind sorts of goodness and there are . . . enlightened sorts of goodness. Women such as ourselves have been living the blind sort. Preparing for nothing but . . . oblivion.

ROSE: *(Flummoxed, scowling.)* Mrs. Wilton. I assure you that I am a most happy individual.

LOTTY: *(Defeated.)* Yes. Of course. Will you believe that I have never in my life spoken like this to anyone?

ROSE: It's the weather, I'm sure.

LOTTY: *(Lost.)* Yes. And the advertisement.

ROSE: Yes.

LOTTY: And both of us being so miserable. *(Sadly.)* Something has been lost, Rose. Something has shifted, and I don't recognize anything anymore.

ROSE: *(Moved.)* We must all deal with loss, Mrs. Wilton. Each in his way.

LOTTY: Yes. That's true. But don't you ever wish you could go back, to hold on tighter? But we can't, can we? We can only go forward. But how? This I haven't seen.

ROSE: Do you see things often, Mrs. Wilton?

LOTTY: Lotty. Yes, I do. *(Defeated.)* But seeing and doing are two different things, aren't they? *(They think.)* "To those who appreciate wisteria and sunshine." *(Lotty smiles wistfully.)* That's you and me, Rose. That much I do see. *(Thunder. Half-light.)*

FEED THE HOLE
Michael Stock

Dramatic
Shelly and Samantha, twenties

*Shelly and Samantha, friends since they were kids, are in a dress shop
trying on outfits and talking about whether or not they are happy
with their lives so far. Samantha and Shelly at a clothing store.
Samantha is trying on dresses. Shelly sits outside the dressing room,
and Samantha is modeling. They have many bags from other stores
with them.*

SAMANTHA: I'm telling you, three years go so quickly.

SHELLY: Three years . . . wow.

SAMANTHA: Right? He's so funny, too. He's all secretive, but I know where
we're going. I might as well have planned it myself. Called for reser-
vations. Bought my gift . . .

SHELLY: What, you're going back to, what's it called, where you had your
first date.

SAMANTHA: Yamaguchi Sushi. Yeah. And this bracelet, oh my God.

SHELLY: He gave it to you already?

SAMANTHA: No, but we were at Tiffany's a couple months ago and I basically told him to get it for me.

SHELLY: That's great.

SAMANTHA: So I'm sure he got it. Yeah, three years. Yours is coming up,
right? That's why you have to be certain, you know?

SHELLY: Do you like this dress, or no? It's beautiful, but — it's —

SAMANTHA: Yeah?

SHELLY: Definitely, try the other one.

SAMANTHA: OK, thanks. I'm just saying. You have to —

SHELLY: Definitely. The other one. The scooping neckline. Lets the girls
breathe a bit. This one's so conservative.

SAMANTHA: You have to leave him.

SHELLY: That's — I'm fine.

SAMANTHA: I want you happy. So get out.

SHELLY: We're working through —

SAMANTHA: With another guy?

SHELLY: I wasn't going to tell you —

SAMANTHA: I'm not judging you, but —

SHELLY: — I knew you'd use it against me.

SAMANTHA: I'm not —

SHELLY: Yes. You are. And fine. You need to. Judge me so your pretty life seems intact. Stays perfect.

SAMANTHA: I'm trying to help —

SHELLY: Judge me so you don't have to admit you or Rob would do the same.

SAMANTHA: I would never let it get to this point. I would've — Break up with Brett.

SHELLY: Well, no, of course you wouldn't let it get to this point. You tell Rob exactly how to act.

SAMANTHA: You bet your ass. But if he did, I'd break it off. If I had a fling. A one-night thing. All drunk and crazy. Fine. But this is ongoing. I'm not saying you are a bad person. Or a wrong person. You've just —

SHELLY: This is the best thing I've ever done.

SAMANTHA: So run off with your new guy. I'm all for it. But what you're doing now — the deception — It's killing me.

SHELLY: It's not about the other —

SAMANTHA: I'm sorry, I can't keep it in. I can't trust you.

SHELLY: It's not about you either.

SAMANTHA: You're not living in a bubble, Shell. You say you're happy now, that's great, but everyone else's hurt.

SHELLY: This is not about you.

SAMANTHA: It is. I looked up to you. When we were kids, you always made the plans. Let's play house. Let's move to New York.

SHELLY: I'm not that girl.

SAMANTHA: No, you're not. But you were. And I envied you. I shouldn't be the one telling you how to act. You should tell me.

SHELLY: Well, I got tired of telling everyone. You. Brett. What about me? I gotta take care of me.

SAMANTHA: So stop trapping yourself in lies, and make a change. I want to help you get back to being that girl. Go to the other guy . . . Or don't leave Brett. Go back and fix it. I don't care which. But do something. Then everything can go back to the way we planned. I mean, hell! You used to plan Barbie weddings!

SHELLY: She's a fucking doll, Sam. She's not real. If she were, she'd be five-nine and a hundred and ten pounds. This is life. It's ugly. It doesn't have a thirty-nine-inch bust and twenty-three inch waist. And I can't fit into that myth anymore.

SAMANTHA: It's not a myth; it's our plan. You find a guy, we raise our kids together —

SHELLY: It's a delusion. I don't want to *be* that girl anymore. There's no Prince Charming. There's no Brett Butler at the bottom of the stairs. And I'm not going to search for some man, some Wizard of Oz, to give my heart and courage back.

SAMANTHA: Look, I don't want to live with a bunch of letters and numbers after my address, and that's what it comes down to. I don't want to be Apartment Six-E my whole life, and neither do you. I want to walk up to my front door and step into my living room. One buzzer. One mailbox. One home. And you're right, I push Rob around. Because he needs me to. He may need some work — he may need my help — but I want him sitting in my living room when I walk in. And that's no delusion. I walk around this city and all I see are babies. Mothers and nannies coming out of their living rooms, and bowling me over with these baby bumper cars. And see those little . . . things — those faces. And I want one. Every time I see one, I want to either steal and run away with it, or smother it. I don't know. But I want one. And so do you.

(Breaths. Blackout.)

FIGHTING WORDS
Sunil Kuruvilla

Dramatic
Nia and Peg

> *Nia and Peg are sisters. They are Welsh. Nia is older than Peg. She
> dreams of becoming a TV reporter. Both of them are fascinated by
> a local boxing hero who is off to America to fight for the world title.
> Mrs. Davies is also in this scene, but says very little.*

NIA: . . . Who are you, Peggy? Every boxer has a nickname, what's yours?
Eh, Peggy? What name will you use when you're in a match? Big *Boxer.*
Boxer Peggy. *(Peg spits on Nia's finger.)*

PEG: Water. I'll be water.

[MRS. DAVIES: Did you get the paper plates?]

PEG: Ohhh.

[MRS. DAVIES: Oh no, Peg — you said you'd get them. I told the women
to bring a chair and fork to the gym and I'd get the plates. The Owens
closed their grocery shop. What are we going to do?]

NIA: Don't worry, Mrs. Davies. I'll get some in Swansea.

[MRS. DAVIES: Thank you, Nia. Ice. *(Mrs. Davies distributes golden syrup
and brush to Nia and Peg.)*]

NIA: You scare him, Peg.

PEG: How's that?

NIA: The first time you met him was at the thimble factory.

PEG: Correct.

NIA: His first day, she came up to him and wouldn't leave him alone.

PEG: Incorrect.

NIA: He was petrified. *(Nia becomes Peg.)* I heard about you. You only stayed
in the ground ten minutes.

[MRS. DAVIES: Good, Nia. Funny.]

PEG: Go on.

NIA: You were scared of the dark.

PEG: All right.

NIA: Did you cry?

PEG: *(Becomes Johnny.)* Yes.

[MRS. DAVIES: What else —]

NIA: All the men in this town work the mines.

PEG: Not me.

NIA: You don't mind being in a room full of women?

PEG: No.

NIA: You should know some things about this place. Don't drift off. That's when mistakes happen. We'll have to talk to each other to stay awake.

PEG: I don't talk much.

NIA: You will with me.

PEG: No.

NIA: Oh yes. You don't and I'll have you talk to my sister Nia. She's the smartest person I know. Could teach a cat to bark she could. This is a hard enough forehead as it is. *[Translates: This job is hard enough as it is.]* What's your name then?

PEG: Johnny.

NIA: Every flack in this town's a "Johnny."

PEG: Thimbles. We risk our hands so others can protect their fingers. *(Peg strikes a boxing pose and examines her hands.)*

NIA: You're the boxer. Johnny Owen!

PEG: You're surprised. Most are.

NIA: I want to box. Take me to the gym. Please. I'll do anything. You have to, have to, have to. *(Nia crowds into Peg's face, throwing ridiculous punches to mock her sister. Peg backs away.)*

PEG: No, Nia. It wasn't like that. I was quiet. It was Johnny's idea. I told him the men would never let me in the gym but he insisted. He said to me: *(Peg becomes Johnny.)* What's your name, then?

NIA: *(Becomes Peg, acts slow.)* Peg. Peg Parret. That would be my name.

PEG: I just met you, Peg, but already I like you.

NIA: But I'm so dummmb —

PEG: You and me are the same, Peg. I can tell.

NIA: *(Becomes herself.)* You're not a full yard.

PEG: No, I mean it. Come to the gym with me. I want you to. I'll show you what I know. I can teach you, Peg. The men won't say anything if you're with me. I want to spend more time with you.

NIA: Johnny doesn't talk like that.

PEG: Does with me. We figure out how to get your man to drop his guard. How to get inside. How to pin him in the corner. We work side by side at the thimble factory — every day, don't forget. We talk so much my mouth gets dry. I have to drink bowls and bowls of water. He never leaves me alone — [Mrs. Davies. What's the matter?]

MRS. DAVIES: Nothing.

PEG: You look like you're going to cry.

MRS. DAVIES: No I don't.

PEG: All right.

MRS. DAVIES: I want to show you something. I've got a surprise for Mr. Davies. He has no idea. *(Mrs. Davies exits.)*]

PEG: Poor woman.

NIA: Has she ever said anything to you?

PEG: No.

NIA: She pretends everything's fine. Deep down she must know.

PEG: Nia.

NIA: What?

PEG: I know Johnny's hands. *(Silence. Peg slowly starts to confess her relationship with Johnny to her sister.)* Every Saturday night, Johnny and I meet in the basement of the church with the rest of you. We wait until everyone starts dancing close then we sneak away. We go to the gym. I boost Johnny to the window. I can't fit through but he can. He comes around and unlocks the door. You don't want to hear the rest.

NIA: I can. Tell me.

PEG: Johnny never likes to take his shirt off. I have to go first. My skirt. His trousers. My stockings. His socks. Stripped naked, we dress each other. Working from the ground up. Socks, shoes. Leather cup. The laces rub my spine. Satin trunks tied in the front. The knot against my belly. Fingers on my lips. His rough hands rub Vaseline on my face.

NIA: Then what?

PEG: We try to make each other bleed. Eyes wide open. Seeing everything. I'm bigger but he's quicker. I try to get inside on him, close the distance. I make him go hard: *(Shouts:)* "Don't hold back! Floor me! Go for my body!" *(Peg moves toward Nia.)* Hook to the kidney. Shot to the belly. He makes me ache. But I study his body. He drops his shoulder after double jabbing. He sits down on his back foot. He always backs away shocked when I figure him out. In the end we come together. A tired clinch. *(Peg clinches Nia.)* Shoulder to shoulder. Our arms hooked together to keep the other from punching. Breathing each other's breath. Exhausted. Alive. You hear your man breathe. You hear yourself.

NIA: *(Shares her feelings.)* We have a spot in the hills. Near the canal. We went there every night the week before he left. We stayed there until the cut of dawn, lying in the wet grass, leaving our marks on the ground. *(Peg lets go of Nia, backs away.)*

PEG: What were you doing there?

NIA: Keeping him awake, getting him used to American time. I talked and talked. He listened until my voice was gone. He drifted off and I watched him get bigger. The crotch of his pants growing from whatever he was dreaming about.

PEG: Did you touch him?

NIA: No.

PEG: Did you?

NIA: No. *(Beat.)* I didn't. I'm not that kind of girl. I covered him with my dress. Two girls on the hills. One asleep. The other wide awake, shivering in her slip. All you have is the boxing.

PEG: And what do you have?

NIA: He tells me his secrets.

PEG: His secrets. And what would those be?

NIA: He keeps a diary. Did you know that? He writes in it every morning. Night before a fight he dreams he gets thumbed in the eye and can't see.

PEG: What else did he tell you?

NIA: He gets bumps on his head before a fight. Nerves.

PEG: You're lying.

NIA: If you took off the gloves you could feel them.

PEG: Did George know you were there?

NIA: He did.

PEG: If I was your husband I wouldn't let you lie in the grass with another man.

NIA: I was helping Johnny.

PEG: I don't care.

NIA: Saturday, September 20, 1980. Last night in Los Angeles, Johnny Owen lost a split decision in his attempt to win the world bantamweight title from Champion Lupe Pintor. When asked about the fight, Owen replied, "I am disappointed but I will get on with my life. I am retiring now and I do so making one request. I ask that Peg Parret leave me alone." I am Nia Parret for BBC Radio Swansea.

FIVE FLIGHTS
Adam Bock

Dramatic
Jane and Olivia

> *Jane's husband and her brother and sister-in-law have inherited a*
> *spectacular aviary from their father, who has recently passed away.*
> *Olivia, a friend of her sister-in-law, has an idea about what to do*
> *with it.*

JANE: He left the aviary to us. To all three of us, actually. Well I mean to
the three kids, to Adele and of course to Ed and to Bobby. Which
means in some ways to me. Well. To me, really, also, since what is
mine is Bobby's and what is Bobby's is mine.

OLIVIA: He said he doesn't care what happens to it.

JANE: Ed said that?

OLIVIA: No Bobby did.

JANE: Bobby never said that.

OLIVIA: He said he didn't care.

JANE: Oh no Bobby cares.

OLIVIA: That's what he said.

JANE: Why you care what happens to it?

OLIVIA: I'm helping Adele. Decide. What to do.

JANE: Adele should decide for herself.

OLIVIA: She asked me. As a friend. To help her.

JANE: The will said "Three agreeing would be best. But two can decide."
Three being Adele and Ed and Bobby. Not Adele and Ed and Bobby
and Olivia.

OLIVIA: Or Jane.

JANE: Two being Bobby and Adele. Or Bobby and Ed.

OLIVIA: Or Adele and Ed. Since Bobby doesn't care.

JANE: Oh. Bobby cares. A lot.

OLIVIA: He told Adele "Take it." "I don't want the old thing." "I hate that place." "I hate the smell."

JANE: Bobby loved his mother. He loves this place.

OLIVIA: Bobby doesn't love this place. Adele told me he said "Take it. Take it!"

JANE: When did he say this?

OLIVIA: Adele said "He was so loud." "Take it!" she said he said.

JANE: When did he supposedly say this?

OLIVIA: After the funeral. When they were alone. In the dining room.

JANE: He was upset.

OLIVIA: Of course he was upset. But Jane. That doesn't mean he was lying.

JANE: That was the wrong time to talk to him. He was upset. She shouldn't have been talking to him about things like that at a time like that.

OLIVIA: It sounds like that's what Bobby wants.

JANE: No.

OLIVIA: Doesn't it?

JANE: That's not what Bobby wants.

OLIVIA: That's not what you want.

JANE: OK. *(Long pause.)* Because what I want. *(Long pause.)* Is what Bobby wants. *(Pause.)* Too. *(Long pause.)* That's how we work. *(Pause.)* Bobby thinks we should sell it.

OLIVIA: You want to sell it?

JANE: It's worth a lot of money. Someone should build something reasonable out there. Houses or. Condos or. Something useful. Something new. Something clean. Something clean someone new could use.

OLIVIA: I want to build out there.

JANE: This land would be perfect for a house.

OLIVIA: I want to rebuild out here.

JANE: It's so close to town, but with air and trees. It's attractive. People are attracted to this spot.

OLIVIA: This is a holy place.

JANE: Someone could work magic out here.

OLIVIA: This isn't a place to develop. This is a place that already is.

JANE: Olivia. It's an old aviary. It's crumbling. Look at the paint. Look at the broken glass. The wood is splitting. It's covered in bird shit. It's unsafe. The birds are all gone. The plants are all dead. It's done.

OLIVIA: It's not done.

JANE: It is.

OLIVIA: It's not done.

JANE: It's old.

OLIVIA: It's tired. It needs care.

JANE: It's not holy.

OLIVIA: It's still awake.

JANE: Its back is broken. It's done.

OLIVIA: Your heart's broken that's what's broken. *(Pause.)* Adele's father loved this place. So he got old. So he let some of it fall down. So. We shouldn't tear the rest of it down. We should push it back up.

JANE: I'm not interested in your holy-roller stuff.

OLIVIA: That's where the pulpit is going to be.

JANE: Oh. Is that what Adele wants?

OLIVIA: No. That's what I want. Adele wants it over there. People will sit here. On pleasant days, on benches, under the trees. The birds will come back. We'll need a parking lot.

JANE: A parking lot?

OLIVIA: Big enough for our church.

JANE: Your church for the birds.

OLIVIA: You'd have house and house and house

JANE: No. I'd have one nice new house.

OLIVIA: And house and car and house and house

JANE: Maybe two. Something clean.

OLIVIA: I want. A church that would soar. For the glory of.

JANE: It's ridiculous. A waste. Of space. And of listening.

OLIVIA: Ridiculous is thinking the spirit doesn't matter. Jane.

JANE: Oh the spirit matters. Olivia. But I'm quite sure that what you're describing would house a spirit completely unlike any I would ever care for.

. . . IN THE ABSENCE OF SPRING . . .

Joe Calarco

Dramatic
Christina and Elaine, thirties

> *Christina: comes from money — old money — so no need or incli-*
> *nation to announce it to the world; she simply wears it well. A doc-*
> *umentary filmmaker. Elaine: the life of the party. Everyone loves her.*
> *Smokes a lot, drinks a lot, and looks cool doing it. A phone sex op-*
> *erator. Elaine wants to leave New York and is searching for some*
> *place to go. Christina has just had a disturbing encounter. A bar.*
> *Elaine drinks as she peruses a huge map laid out in front of her.*

ELAINE: Equatorial Guinea! Equatorial Guinea? Equatorial Guinea. I know
— I know — I know this
(*Christina runs in breathless and shaken. She needs a drink.*)

CHRISTINA: Give me something . . . ummm — well — ummm . . . something very strong.

ELAINE: Hey! (*No response from Christina.*) O — K — (*To bartender.*) Hey
Jim Bob, ya ever hear of Equatorial Guinea? I know it's here somewhere. Damn. I remember it very distinctly from like the fourth grade.
Maybe they like changed the name. Like what they did with Zimbabwe. I mean, all through school, as long as I can remember, it was
called . . . something else. And then one day in like eighth grade,
"BAM!" Zimbabwe. And I just thought, "Well, Jesus. Somebody has
to go and change all the maps." (*Finding another location.*) Tahiti! . . .
Naw. Lichtensteen — stein. Paraguay. Paraguay? Paraguay. That seems
like a place. Paraguay.

CHRISTINA: Joseph Mengele lived there.

ELAINE: Excuse me.

CHRISTINA: Joseph Mengele. For years. Hiding away.

ELAINE: I thought it was Brazil. Like in "The Boys From."

CHRISTINA: Well, later. But Paraguay was first.

ELAINE: Hm.

CHRISTINA: You know they only found his body about ten years ago.

ELAINE: Really?

CHRISTINA: Only ten years of proof. Of scientific fact finally revealing the truth. But before that? I mean, decades of survivors and descendants tossing and turning, not truly knowing. Well, yeah — speculation — probability. But I am sorry, until bones are found, and — and DNA, and tufts of hair. I mean, without those things, they must have just lain there sleepless. For decades. Thinking that there was an actual possibility that evil still walked the earth.

CHRISTINA: Don't go there. It would seem — . . . Well, a place that had harbored such a thing seems . . . well . . .

ELAINE: Yes.

(Christina raises her glass to Elaine.)

CHRISTINA: Christina.

(Elaine raises her glass to Christina.)

ELAINE: Elaine.

CHRISTINA: So Elaine, what do you do that you can possibly head to Paraguay or Tahiti or wherever?

ELAINE: Oh, this and that.

CHRISTINA: Oh.

ELAINE: Odd . . . odd jobs.

CHRISTINA: Like what?

ELAINE: Well . . .

CHRISTINA: I'm sorry — . . .

ELAINE: No —

CHRISTINA: No —

ELAINE: You didn't —

CHRISTINA: Really —

ELAINE: It's not a —

CHRISTINA: I should just —

ELAINE: No —

CHRISTINA: I'll just —

ELAINE: Phone sex!

CHRISTINA: What?

ELAINE: Phone sex. I'm a — a phone sex operator.

CHRISTINA: Really.

ELAINE: Yeah.

CHRISTINA: Really? *(Pause.)* What do you say?

ELAINE: Excuse me?

CHRISTINA: What do you say to . . . well, the callers.

ELAINE: Oh come on — . . .

CHRISTINA: No really. I'm intensely curious.

ELAINE: I — . . . No, I —

CHRISTINA: Please.

ELAINE: Really?

CHRISTINA: Really.

ELAINE: OK . . . ummm . . . this is so weird . . . OK . . . well, first I might say something like, well, like "You wanna fuck me? Don't ya? You know you wanna fuck me. Come on, fuck me. Please . . . Please . . . Please . . ." *(Pause.)* Something like that.

CHRISTINA: I see.

ELAINE: Yeah.

CHRISTINA: But is it ever — . . . well you know what I mean. Do you ever get, you know, —

ELAINE: No. Never.

CHRISTINA: Well is it ever — is it ever you know like — well just — . . .

ELAINE: No. Never.

CHRISTINA: Well, do you ever get —

ELAINE: No.

CHRISTINA: Never?

ELAINE: Never. I don't feel a thing.

CHRISTINA: Hm.

ELAINE: Not once. *(Pause.)*

CHRISTINA: Me neither.

IZ SHE IZZY OR IZ HE AIN'TZY OR IZ THEY BOTH

Lonnie Carter

Comic
Isabella and Suzy, teens to twenties

> *This two-character scene is from 'Iz She Izzy or Iz He Ain'tzy or Iz They Both,' a screwball murder mystery resolving the death of Isabella Borgward, at the hands, perhaps, of Justice "Choo-Choo" Justice. Age of characters — this play has been performed by high school and college students and professionals. In other words, youngsters or anywhere up. This is the first time we see Isabella Borgward, to be joined shortly by Suzy Quzer, his Girl Thursday. Isabella Borgward's office. Isabella is clearly played by the actor playing Choo-Choo.*

ISABELLA: *(On the phone.)* Hello, Bingo? No? Bingo's calling numbers? OK, give me Bongo . . . Bongo's playing Bingo? How many cards does he have? G-46 and he's got three ways? I hope Bongo doesn't get beat. My best of Bingo to Bongo. Tell him I got two cards for the next game. Let me have Bango . . . Bango's what? . . . Started a rival game of Bango rivaling neighborhood Bingo? No. Call the Bungo Squad. I suppose Bengo's not available. . . Oh, he is. Well, you tell Bengo to call Bungo, hit Bango, cheer Bongo and pay Bingo. Get my lingo? By the way, Jingo, how come you're free to answer the phone? . . . Oh, that's how you play dingaling. *(She hangs up.)*

I'm Isabella Borgward
Editor-publisher of *Skin*
The magazine that's beauty-deep
I'm Isabella Borgward
Boss of Gloss

(Singing.)

Skin's *real*
Feel
Pages of Skin
Are pages of skin
Torn from actual flesh
Born of supple nitties
Enormous gritties
We're bumpy
We're grindy
Come lose your mindy

Don't peep
Skin-*dive*

Skin *is so into skin*
It's bone

So buy Skin
Love Skin
Adore Skin

'Cause it's by skin
Of skin
And for skin

I'm Isabella Borgward

And somebody's out to kill me.
(Enter Suzy Quzer.)
SUZY: *(Singing.) I've been sailing along*
 This moonlit day
 On the sauce I'm ever after
 This moonlit day
ISABELLA: Suzy, you've got to help me.
SUZY: Izzy, Izzy, ask me for help. Ask me, Izzy, ask me. I'll help for the asking, Izzy. Help help. Ask, Izzy, ask.

ISABELLA: I beg your pardon?

SUZY: Izzy, Izzy, ask me for help. Ask me, Izzy, ask me.

ISABELLA: Help!

SUZY: What is it, Izzy?

ISABELLA: Will you stop calling me Izzy?

SUZY: That's the help you ask for? Not calling you Izzy is a help?

ISABELLA: Suzy.

SUZY: Don't call me "Suzy."

ISABELLA: What am I supposed to call you?

SUZY: What am I supposed to call you?

ISABELLA: I asked you first.

SUZY: Don't call me.

ISABELLA: I'll call you.

SUZY: Call me and I'll call you.

ISABELLA: Help!

SUZY: Ask me, Izzy, ask me.

ISABELLA: I need a boost.

SUZY: Give me your left foot.

ISABELLA: Which one?

SUZY: Didn't you hear me, I said "Give me your left foot."

ISABELLA: Which one?

SUZY: Two left feet, huh? Well, give me your right foot.

ISABELLA: Make up your mind, here's my left foot.

SUZY: That's your right foot.

ISABELLA: What's wrong with that?

SUZY: Afraid I won't hold you up?

ISABELLA: You're no bandit.

SUZY: Stick up both your feet and reach for the sky.

ISABELLA: I will not. I'm taking a long walk off a short pier.

SUZY: May I come along?

ISABELLA: Lead the way.

SUZY: What about the boost?

ISABELLA: Help!

SUZY: Help has arrived.

ISABELLA: Somebody's out to kill me.

JULY 7, 1994
Donald Margulies

Dramatic
Kate, thirties; Ms. Pike, thirties

> *This scene takes place in a medical clinic. Kate is removing*
> *stitches from the palm of Ms. Pike's hand. Ms. Mike is black, in*
> *her thirties, five-months pregnant.*

MS. PIKE: Oww!

KATE: Sorry. *(Ms. Pike groans in pain.)* I'm trying not to hurt you. I'm
sorry.

MS. PIKE: How many more you got?

KATE: Just a few. *(Pause.) What* happened exactly?

MS. PIKE: Hmm?

KATE: *How'd* you hurt your hand?

MS. PIKE: I told you, I don't know, I cut it.

KATE: How?

MS. PIKE: Kitchen.

KATE: Yeah, I know, how?

MS. PIKE: Accident. *You* know. Damn! Could you not hurt me so much?

KATE: I'm sorry.

MS. PIKE: This gonna take long? 'Cause I got to pick up my daughter.

KATE: I just need to dress it; there's some infection. *(Silence while she at-*
tends to her.) So, have you been following this O.J. thing?

MS. PIKE: Oh, yeah, are you kidding? There's nothing else on. Day and
night. I'm really getting sick of it, too: O.J., O.J., O.J. . . .

KATE: So what do you think?

MS. PIKE: What do I think?, you mean did he do it?

KATE: Yeah, do you think he did it?

MS. PIKE: Nah, I think it's all a frame-up.

KATE: You do? Really?

MS. PIKE: Oh, yeah. You can be sure, a famous *white* man, they find *his* wife dead, they ain't gonna be all over *him.*

KATE: Oh, I don't know, a history of abuse? I'm sure the ex-husband is the first one they look for, no matter who he is.

MS. PIKE: *(Over "who he is.")* Did anybody see him do it?

KATE: Well . . .

MS. PIKE: *(Continuous.)* Did anybody *see* him? No. How do you know it wasn't some mugger who did it? Hmm? How do you know it wasn't someone out to *get* O.J.? You don't know that and neither do I. It could've been some Charles Manson thing. You don't know.

KATE: Do you think the judge is going to allow that evidence?

MS. PIKE: She better not.

KATE: Why?!

MS. PIKE: It's illegal! The cops broke the law when they hopped the wall! They had no right!

KATE: Don't you think they had just cause for entering the premises? The Bronco was on the street.

MS. PIKE: *(Over "The Bronco . . .")* They didn't have a warrant! They had no warrant! They can't just break into somebody's house . . .

KATE: But the circumstantial evidence is pretty overwhelming, don't you think? I mean, don't you think there's sufficient cause for him to stand trial?

MS. PIKE: Those L.A. cops, they just want to get themselves one more nigger.

KATE: Why would they want to get O.J. Simpson?

MS. PIKE: Why?! *Why?!* Honey, what country do *you* live in? *(Beat.)*

KATE: But I think you're confusing the issue; the issue is not about race.

MS. PIKE: Not about race? Sure it's about race. Everything's about race. *This* is about race. *(Meaning their exchange. Beat.)*

KATE: Maybe I'm hopelessly naïve.

MS. PIKE: Maybe you are. Maybe you are. *(Beat.)* I don't know, all I know is, if he *did* do it, if he *did,* you can be sure she pushed him.

KATE: Pushed him?, how do you mean?

MS. PIKE: *Pushed* him. I bet she got him so mad . . . her with her sexy clothes, waving her titties around, hanging out with those pretty boy models. I bet she got him plenty mad with her ways.

KATE: What ways?

MS. PIKE: Screwing around. She screwed everything in sight, that girl.

KATE: How do you know?

MS. PIKE: She was a tramp. That's what they say.

KATE: Who says?

MS. PIKE: All the papers. That's what you read. She drove him crazy with jealousy. That was her hold on him. I know women like this. That's how they keep their men. My sister is like this.

KATE: But she was trying to break away. She was finally on her own. It's classic, you know, when battered women —

MS. PIKE: Who said she was battered? You don't know. How do you know that? You don't know what goes on in the privacy of their own home.

KATE: *(Continuous, over the above.)* — break away, when they finally break away, that's when their husbands lose it, that's when they get killed. The cops were called to their house on several occasions, she said she was afraid he was going to kill her.

MS. PIKE: Yeah?, if she was so afraid, she should've gotten the hell out of town.

KATE: Oh, come on —

MS. PIKE: She should've moved.

KATE: *(Continuous, over the above.)* — take her kids out of school, away from their family and friends? He would've tracked her down anywhere.

MS. PIKE: Ah, she was too busy spending his money to leave. Too busy shopping Beverly Hills.

KATE: Did you hear that 911 tape?

MS. PIKE: Yeah, I heard it.

KATE: And? What did you think about that?

MS. PIKE: What do I think? I think they had a fight. So what? Lots of folks have fights. Doesn't mean he killed her.

KATE: Yeah, but you heard it. That was rage, pure and simple. She was terrified.

MS. PIKE: I heard the reason he was so mad? He walked in on her and some guy going down on him in the living room.

KATE: Where'd you hear that?

MS. PIKE: Waiting in line Stop 'n' Shop, one of those papers. They got sound experts to pick up what he's yelling in the background? He was yelling about her and this guy Keith.

KATE: Who's Keith?

MS. PIKE: *(Shrugs.)* Some guy she was cheating with.

KATE: Wait a second, they were already divorced. She was his ex-wife, she could have sex with whomever she liked. That's not cheating. She was a single woman. And what if she *did* have sex with these guys? Does that mean she deserved to be bludgeoned to death because she was promiscuous? *(Ms. Pike makes a scoffing sound; beat.)* What are you saying? She deserved it? *(Silence.)*

MS. PIKE: All I'm saying . . . O.J. had no business marrying her in the first place. *If* you know what I mean. *(Silence.)*

KATE: When your boyfriend hits *you,* do *you* deserve it?

MS. PIKE: What?! Who said my boyfriend hits me?

(Kate looks at her as if to say, You can level with me. Long pause.)

It's not the same.

KATE: Why not?

MS. PIKE: Oh, man . . .

KATE: Why isn't it?

MS. PIKE: 'Cause it's not, OK? *(Beat.)* We got into a fight about the kids, that's all.

KATE: What about the kids?

MS. PIKE: I don't know, he started yelling at them about something. I got worried.

KATE: What were you worried about?

MS. PIKE: I was worried he might hit them.

KATE: Why was he yelling at them?

MS. PIKE: What are all these questions? They were bad, OK?

KATE: Uh-huh. What were they doing that was so bad?

MS. PIKE: Yelling and screaming and stuff. You know. Talking back.

KATE: Does he hit the kids? I mean, generally?

MS. PIKE: Sometimes.

KATE: Does he hit them hard?

MS. PIKE: Sometimes he'll smack them around, yeah.

KATE: What do you mean by smack them around?

MS. PIKE: Smack them around, *you* know.

KATE: Does he smack them? Or punch them?

MS. PIKE: Yeah, smack them, punch them. Just to scare them, you know?

KATE: Uh-huh. And does he?

MS. PIKE: Oh, yeah! Sometimes, he'll, *you* know, *use* things.

KATE: Use things? What do you mean?

MS. PIKE: Throw things. *You* know, plates, stuff, whatever's there. Once he threw the cat at my son.

KATE: The cat?!

MS. PIKE: *(Continuous.)* Didn't like the way he talked to him?, picked up the cat?, right across the room. I couldn't believe it. You should've seen: scratches all over his face and stuff.

KATE: Sounds pretty bad.

MS. PIKE: *(Shrugs.)* He got the message, though, my son.

KATE: I don't know . . . Seems to me there are other ways of getting the message across.

MS. PIKE: You got to do *some*thing. I mean, when he hits them, they deserve it. Oh, man, they deserve it all right.

KATE: Why do they deserve it?

MS. PIKE: They're out of control. You should see. They are out of control. They need discipline. They need it. My father did it. Otherwise, you know how kids get, they walk all over you. Somebody's got to take control, show them who's the boss.

KATE: So you were worried he was going to hit the kids, but you say they deserved it? I don't get it.

MS. PIKE: *(Over "get it.")* I was worried he'd get carried away. *You* know.

KATE: Are they his kids?

MS. PIKE: No, no. *This* one's his, though. *(Meaning her pregnancy.)*

KATE: I see. *(Beat.)* So, you got into a fight over the kids, he picked up a knife, started waving it around, and you got cut.

MS. PIKE: It was an accident. He didn't mean it.

KATE: No, you just happened to walk into it.

MS. PIKE: He was mad. He just wanted to scare me.

KATE: "Scare" you? Does he hit you a lot?

MS. PIKE: No! Not a lot. Sometimes. Sometimes he'll, you know, give me a punch I do something he don't like.

KATE: Like what? What could you possibly do to warrant a punch?

MS. PIKE: *(Over "to warrant a punch?")* Could be anything. What I cooked, what I say. He don't like it when I talk back.

KATE: That sounds pretty difficult. *(Ms. Pike shrugs.)* I mean, you never know when you might set him off.

MS. PIKE: Oh, I have a pretty good idea.

KATE: He just went after you with a knife!

MS. PIKE: *(Shrugs.)* Yeah, well . . . I interfered —

KATE: You what?!

MS. PIKE: *(Continuous.)* — I shouldn't've.

KATE: Is that what he told you?

MS. PIKE: No, it's the truth. I should've butt out. It was none of my business. He had words with the kids, I should've butt out.

KATE: *(Over "I should've butt out.")* They're your children! Ms. Pike! This man is abusing you and your children!

MS. PIKE: What, you're gonna lecture me now?

KATE: Why would you, why would *any*one deserve to be hit?

MS. PIKE: In his eyes I do.

KATE: I'm not talking about his eyes.

MS. PIKE: I mean, the way he sees it, I do something pisses him off — wham.

KATE: Yeah, but do you feel you deserve it?

MS. PIKE: I'm used to it by now.

KATE: That's not what I'm asking.

MS. PIKE: It's the way it is. If that's the way it has to be . . .

KATE: It doesn't have to be that way, there are people you can talk to, you know, agencies.

MS. PIKE: *(Over "agencies.")* Shit . . .

KATE: *(Continuous.)* I can walk you over to meet someone right here at the clinic, I can introduce you to someone right now.

MS. PIKE: *(Over "right now.")* What, so they'd tell me to leave him? Tell me to walk out on him? *Then* what? Then what happens to me? What happens to my kids? Look, lady, you don't know *me*. You don't know a *damn* thing about my life.

KATE: True enough.

MS. PIKE: I came for you to take out my stitches. *(Kate nods. A beat. While writing a prescription, back to business:)*

KATE: Here's an antibiotic for that infection. Three times a day for ten days with meals. And try to keep that hand dry. *(Kate rips the prescription off the pad, hands it to her.)*

LIVING OUT

Lisa Loomer

Dramatic
Nancy, late twenties to midthirties; Ana, about thirty

> *Nancy and her husband have recently had a baby. Both of them have very demanding jobs (Nancy's a lawyer). They have hired Ana, Hispanic and an illegal alien, as their nanny. Ana arrives for work, holding handpicked flowers.*

ANA: Oh — you surprise me! I thought you was at your yoga class — *(She puts the flowers in a little vase as Nancy keeps looking in the cabinet.)*

NANCY: No. *(Beat.)* I hate yoga. Frankly, I find lying on the floor listening to the breathing of thirty women who are in better shape than I am extremely stressful. *(Nancy bangs around some more.)* Do we have any aspirin?

ANA: I put it in the medicine cabinet in the bathroom. *(Ana goes off to get it. Reminds her.)* We got to get the childproofing for the cabinets, Nancy, it's very dangerous now that Jenna is crawling —

NANCY: *(Guilty.)* I now. I promise I'll call this weekend.

ANA: Can I get you something else? Chamomile tea?

NANCY: Oh, no thanks, it's just a cold. I must have caught something on the plane. I just hope I haven't given it to Jenna. She seems, I don't know, fussy —

ANA: I could make her some tea too —

NANCY: Tea? For a baby?

ANA: I always give it to my — *(Quickly.)* both my kids — when they were babies in El Salvador. But you can call the doctor if you don't —

NANCY: Oh Ana, please, I trust you. Make me some tea too. But no sugar. And don't sneak any in — *(Ana looks at her.)* I'm kidding!

ANA: I knew that! *(Ana puts the flowers on the table.)*

NANCY: What're these for? God, I didn't forget my own birthday, did I?

ANA: I just thought . . . maybe you like flowers . . . *(Nancy's eyes well up.)* I didn't buy them — I just picked them on the street — *(Nancy starts to cry.)*

NANCY: It's not that. It's just . . . so kind of you. It was just a — really kind thing to do. I'm sorry, I don't know why. I'm — I didn't get much sleep . . . Jenna was so fussy, and nothing — nothing I did seemed to . . . She just kept crying and crying and crying . . . Richard says she never does that with you . . . He thinks she's angry I'm gone so much — *(Laughs/cries.)* Well, clearly *he's* angry — you can always tell when he gets really *nice* . . . What am I saying, he has a right to be angry —

(Ana doesn't know what to say so she says what Nancy has said to her.)

ANA: Well, you got your rights as a woman, Nancy —

NANCY: *(Laughs/cries.)* Rights? I have the right to do it all — and not do any of it very well?

ANA: I know. You got stress —

NANCY: No, *you've* got stress. I mean, you don't even get to see your kids! You know what I should do? I should just call up right now. I should just call up and quit and take care of my own child.

ANA: *(Shocked; blurts.)* Oh no. No Nancy!

NANCY: *(Taken aback.)* Wow. You must think I'm a really lousy mother —

ANA: No!

NANCY: I was joking, Ana —

ANA: Oh —

NANCY: *(Utterly vulnerable.)* But tell me the truth, because I'd quit in a minute — in a second if I thought . . . I mean, I am her mother — I can fuck her up for life!

(Ana thinks. She decides, for a variety of reasons, but mostly for the sake of her own children . . .)

ANA: You're a good mother, Nancy. And Jenna is . . . a very lucky child.

NANCY: I *do* like to work! I like to work — *and* I love my child! Is that so horrible of me?

ANA: You know what? I like to work too! Ay, don't tell that to my husband. Because, in my country, all the women is suppose to love to stay home. I get depressed if I stay home all the time!

NANCY: I know! I know!

ANA: I tell you a secret, I want to go back to school — *(Quickly adds.)* When Jenna is older —

NANCY: You should! You're a smart woman. *(Puts an arm around her.)* You should go to school and get a real job! Thank you. Thank you, Ana.

ANA: Ay dios, I forgot the tea!

(Ana goes and pours tea.)

NANCY: Aren't you having some?

ANA: OK.

(Nancy takes cigarettes from her purse. She opens a window and lights up.)

NANCY: I don't do this in front of Jenna, by the way. *(Confidentially.)* Or Richard.

(Nancy sits. Ana gets her tea but doesn't sit.)

NANCY: *(Laughs.)* Oh, Ana, sit!

ANA: OK.

(An awkward moment when the two of them are actually seated together at the table.)

NANCY: What the hell, let's have some cookies.

(Nancy jumps up, gets a bag of cookies, and offers it to Ana who takes a cookie.)

NANCY: *(Embarrassed.)* Jeez, I certainly didn't mean to get into all that. Let's talk about your life for a change. What's happening with your papers?

ANA: I got my appointment with the immigration next month!

NANCY: That's terrific! And you know what? When your kids come, we're having a party. *(Shakes her hips.)* Et El Cholo.

(Ana feels so awful that she starts to tell Nancy the truth about Santiago.)

ANA: Nancy . . . I . . . I want to tell you something. It's a little bit hard. I should have told you before . . .

(The phone rings.)

ANA: It's about my kids . . .

(The phone rings.)

NANCY: They need something?

ANA: No, no —

(The phone rings again, the machine picks up.)

NANCY'S VOICE ON MACHINE: Hi! You've reached Nancy, Richard, and Jenna. Please leave a message.

NANCY: Maybe I just better listen to the —

(Ana nods.)

DIANE'S VOICE ON MACHINE: Nancy, it's Diane calling around eight twenty-seven. It's important, and I'm in the car, so call my cell if you get this before nine —

(Nancy rolls her eyes at Ana.)

NANCY: Maybe I just better —

(Ana nods. Nancy races to the phone.)

DIANE'S VOICE ON MACHINE: After that I'll be at Disney —

NANCY: *(Into phone; instantly professional.)* Diane? Hi, I just walked in . . . Tonight? Gee, I don't know. I had made plans . . . *(Torn.)* He did? Dinner? . . . No, no, I understand . . . Can you hold just a sec —? *(She covers the mouthpiece and goes to Ana.)*

NANCY: Ana . . . do you think you could possibly do me a huge favor and work late tonight?

ANA: Tonight?

NANCY: I know — it's ridiculously short notice —

ANA: I'm really sorry, Nancy. I can't.

NANCY: *(Surprised.)* You can't?

ANA: I already got plans.

NANCY: Oh gee. I'm sorry . . . *(Beat.)* Ana, I know it's awful of me to ask — but could you possibly change them? For the weekend maybe? I'm home all weekend —

ANA: I don't think so.

NANCY: Well, can you tell me what it is? Maybe I can figure a way to —

ANA: No. *(Beat.)* It's a — a family thing.

NANCY: *(In a bind.)* Oh God — *(Into phone.)* Diane? . . . I'm so sorry. I'll have to call you right back. *(She hangs up.)*

ANA: Please don't be angry —

NANCY: No, no, I understand. It's just — this director is just impossible to pin down —

ANA: *(Feeling cornered.)* I already worked the overtime for the thousand dollars . . . *(She puts her cookie down.)*

NANCY: I know that! But Richard's working late — there's really no one else I can call —

ANA: And Jenna is getting a cold —

NANCY: *(Torn.)* I know. I know . . . But trust me, my boss doesn't want to hear about Jenna . . . and she'll be asleep practically the whole time. I'm sure I'll be back by nine. And then I don't have a trip planned for quite a while . . . *(Sits.)* I wouldn't ask if I didn't really need your help, Ana. What if we say sixty dollars for the four hours — ?

ANA: It's not the money!

NANCY: *(Continued.)* Well, could you possibly just do me a — favor? Just this one time? *(Touches her hand.)* As a . . . a friend?
(Ana hesitates for several moments.)

ANA: I . . . guess I could call my husband . . .
(She starts to get her cell from her bag.)

NANCY: Could you? Oh thank you, Ana, so much. Oh please — use our phone.
(Ana nods and goes to the phone. Nancy goes to the other room.)

ANA: *(Into phone.)* Bobby? Listen, the senora asked me to work late . . . I know I promised, but I'll see his next game . . . *(Angry because she's in such a bind.)* Porque she got no one else! Please — tell him I'll take him to play soccer on the weekend, tell him I don't got to work all weekend! *(Listens, upset.)* Que — you can't go? . . . OK, OK, you got to work too, entiendo . . . *(Unsure.)* Your sister? . . . *(Hesitates.)* Just make sure she know how to get there — and she got his bag, everything —
(Nancy re-enters.)

ANA: *(Continued. Into phone; lighter.)* And tell everybody have a good time at the party! Gracias, mi amor . . . Bye.
(Ana hangs up.)

NANCY: You can? Oh, thank you so much! Listen, if you get hungry, here's a twenty — *(She puts a twenty on the table. Then decides to add another twenty. Then she sits.)* Now let's just finish our cookies. Diane can just wait! Now what did you want to tell me about your kids?

ANA: Oh. *(Beat; rises.)* I told them I sent the T-shirts and they're really excited.

NANCY: Well — good! Listen, Ana, whatever they need . . . *(Rises.)* I mean, you're really part of the family now . . .

(Nancy reaches out and takes her hand.)

NECESSARY TARGETS
Eve Ensler

Dramatic
J.S., forties to fifties; Zlata, thirties

> *J.S. is an American woman who has volunteered to work at a coun-*
> *seling center in Bosnia for female victims of the terrible war there. Zlata*
> *is one of these women. Outside the barracks. It is early dawn. Zlata*
> *is sitting on a chair. She has been weeping. J.S. enters and feels awk-*
> *ward about interrupting her privacy. It is very quiet.*

J.S.: Hot.

ZLATA: Yes, and hot so late. Usually a breeze comes late.

J.S.: I need a breeze to sleep, the air, the sense of going somewhere.

ZLATA: Yes, the smells. The smells hang. Onion. Old cheese. Garbage. All
hanging like a bad mistake.

J.S.: These are difficult circumstances. I am not accustomed to this.

ZLATA: You look different without your makeup.

J.S.: Yes?

ZLATA: Sad. Not so sure. Are you rich?

J.S.: What?

ZLATA: Are you wealthy?

J.S.: Why do you ask?

ZLATA: Because you are wearing a Christian Dior nightgown in a refugee
camp. Because you were able to take time off from work.

J.S.: This is my work.

ZLATA: Oh, I see, we are work.

J.S.: Does it bother you that I am a therapist?

ZLATA: You never seem to answer questions.

J.S.: No, that is my work.

ZLATA: Do you make more money not answering questions?

J.S.: I am trained not to get in the way.

ZLATA: Of what?

J.S.: Of you.

ZLATA: How would you be in my way?

J.S.: By offering answers. By suggesting too much.

ZLATA: Wouldn't that just be a conversation? Don't people in America have conversations? Or do they only work?

J.S.: People pay me to listen to them.

ZLATA: People must be very lonely in America. *(Pause.)* I do not like the night, not anymore, not since the war. It is hard to sleep. I was rich like you before. My parents were very important people. I sleep now in the place of cows.

J.S.: How do you explain what's happened here? How could your neighbors, friends suddenly behave like this?

ZLATA: I used to think it was the leaders, that men really made this war because of their hunger for power. But now I really believe it's in all of us — this thing, this monster, waiting to be let out. It waits there looking for a reason, a master, an invitation. If we are not aware of it, it can conquer us.

J.S.: Is it true you have such a monster in you, Zlata . . .

ZLATA: Oh, I have my ugliness. For example, I can't stand complainers. You know those people who are never happy, never satisfied. *(Complaining voice.)* It's too hot, it's too slow, but I wanted vanilla ice cream . . . What about you. What could drive you to violence?

J.S.: Oh, I don't know . . .

ZLATA: I think you do. *(They sit awkwardly for a bit.)*

J.S.: Well, I can't stand people who apologize all the time. They make me crazy. I'm sorry — could you pass the salt. I'm sorry, but I seem to have forgotten my wallet.

ZLATA: What about people who borrow things and conveniently forget to return them. They act like you're selfish or crazy if you ask for your book back.

J.S.: What about the people who don't listen. I despise that. People who don't wait for you to finish a sentence, make up what you're thinking for you. They forget what you've told them because they never listened in the first place. They make me nuts.

ZLATA: Shoot them at once.

J.S.: Well, retraining camps maybe.

ZLATA: Pointless. Just shoot them. *(Both of them laugh at themselves. Suddenly, J.S. realizes that Zlata is shaking all over.)*

J.S.: What is it, Zlata?

ZLATA: Don't, don't do that psychiatrist thing with me. Has this all been a technique, a trick to get me to talk?

J.S.: What is it?

ZLATA: You only care about the story, the gory details of the story. That's all any of you want.

J.S.: I want to be your friend.

ZLATA: You don't understand that this happened to us — to real people, we were just like you, we weren't ready for this — nothing in our experience prepared us — there were no signs — we weren't fighting for centuries — it didn't come out of our perverted lifestyle — you all want it to be logical — you want us to be different than you are so you can convince yourselves it wouldn't happen there where you are — that's why you turn us into stories, into beasts, communists, people who live in a strange country and speak a strange language — then you can feel safe, superior. Then afterwards we become freaks, the stories of freaks — fax please — get us one raped Bosnian woman, preferably gang-raped, preferably English-speaking.

J.S.: Teach me, Zlata. Teach me how to help you.

ZLATA: Help. Why do you assume I want your help? You Americans don't know how to stop helping. You move so fast, cleaning things up. Fixing.

J.S.: I am a doctor, Zlata.

ZLATA: I was a doctor too before the war. I was the head of the pediatrics unit in Prijedor's main hospital. Now I am a refugee. Now I stare off at the stars without explanation. I look out at the beet fields and weep for no reason.

SANS-CULOTTES IN THE PROMISED LAND

Kirsten Greenidge

Seriocomic
Lena and Charlotte, mid-twenties, both black

> *Lena works for a very well-off black family as a Nanny for their precocious daughter, Greta, who goes to a progressive school taught by Charlotte. Lights up on the laundry room. Lena on the floor covered by letters of the alphabet. Charlotte sprays the floor with her spray bottle twice.*

CHARLOTTE: *Girrrrl.* This family is *whacked.* This family is *whacked.* I mean they are *gone*, oh my goodness. First I ring the bell for near to an hour before Broomhilda *(Mimics Carrmel, the maid.)* answers the door and I'm like can I *please* talk to Lena, thank you very much — that cousin I have? She's gonna hook you up go-*od.* Literacy is legacy and all that so don't you worry but first I have to finish my story, 'cause *then* when I get into the kitchen the mother's like "Lena's *working*, you know" — *you know* — like we're on some English moor, like she's some Parisian aristo-crat or some such nonsense — I minored in French Studies, I know a thing or two about those French rich people. Got their ass *whooped.* She wants to play some role? OK by me as long as I get a role, too. I'll be a sans-culotte, one of those French workers wanted to overthrow every-thang, you know what I'm saying? Natural rights, natural state; none of this abuse of wealth, of privilege, right? *Right?* *(She looks at Lena.)* Why're you on the floor like that?
> *(Lena brushes the letters off of her and stands.)*

LENA: Laundry.

CHARLOTTE: But did you have an accident or something?

LENA: No.

CHARLOTTE: Why're you covered in their dirty clothes?

LENA: I'm not.

CHARLOTTE: You *are*. . . .

(Lena stands, gathers the letters that have accumulated on the floor and throws them in the washer.)

CHARLOTTE: But we're goin' to free your mind, girl, me and my cousin got to — *(The letters clang in the machine.)* How are you supposed to get work done with a machine that clangs around like that? They probably blame you first chance if something shrinks, if something comes back a little worse for wear when it's not your fault. It's the machine. The system; *their system*. Ah-ha? You know?

LENA: Is this cousin a nice cousin or a mean cousin? I had this piano teacher used to hold pencils under my hands to make me play right. The school sent me to her because I squeezed through into one of those programs. It was supposed to be for the smart ones but I squeezed through. I was a cute one. She sharpened the tops real pointy. So as soon as I played wrong I knew it, I felt it. The instant I felt those tips scratch and dig their way to my skin I knew it didn't matter how cute I was: I'd played wrong, I'd made a mistake: stupid, stupid: silly, silly. Teachers had a way of doing that, if they were mean. So I quit that piano. If teachers aren't nice, I quit.

CHARLOTTE: Well that's why I came here, right? To hook you up with my cousin, right?

LENA: And I won't do any tests. They make it seem like my blood is on the outside. One doctor told my mother I had a vitamin deficiency, that's why the reading is too hard. There was this book I wanted to read when I was in the third grade. About this girl named Ramona. Everyone talked about her. Soon as those vitamins kicked in I was going to read that book cover to cover, even use a bookmark, my grandmom was always sending us bookmarks only I never got to use mine.

CHARLOTTE: See that's what I'm talking about. This is supposed to be the Promised Land and eight-year-old you is stuck lining up books, looking at their pictures instead of being able to read them yourself.

LENA: Yeah.

CHARLOTTE: *(Excited.)* Yeah?

LENA: Yes. This is America, right? I'm supposed to learn how to read, right?

Really do it, no guessing, no making up stories about eyeglasses and stupid stuff like that. No driving around in the dark while some snotty-nosed kid makes fun of you, laughs at you while you're just trying to do your job.

CHARLOTTE: Right?

LENA: With your cousin it's going to work this time. I can feel it. I'm going to read everything I get my hands on. Every little thing. But the first thing's going to be that menu at Chili's. The *whole* menu. I'm sick of going to Chili's and ordering the chicken fried steak. Sometimes I do ask for something else, like I'll get a waiter to read me the specials. Lucky for me I was a cute one. After that cousin, it won't matter what I am because I'll know how to read, really read. Like I should have been taught in the first place, since this is America —

CHARLOTTE: Since this is the *Promised* Land. Or it's supposed to be. But people like you and me get left out in the cold, get left to ring the bell for an hour while they carry on inside their McMansions, while they propagate their precious status quo. Man. These people get me. *(She squirts her spray bottle into the air. The two watch the spray evaporate.)*

SOCCER MOMS
Kathleen Clark

Dramatic
Nancy, early forties; Lynn, early thirties

> Soccer Moms *is a play about three mothers who become friends as*
> *they wait on the sidelines while their kids play or practice soccer.*

NANCY: I'm running this thing next year.

LYNN: *You??* Don't make me laugh. The day you run something, I'll run
up the flag.

NANCY: Well, I may not be the "Blimpie Lunch Mom," but I help sometimes.

LYNN: Oh sure, you can't even give me a straight answer about the Bronx
Zoo.

NANCY: You're not serious.

LYNN: I ask and you say no. You weren't at the auction, you didn't help
hang the art show, you weren't at . . .

NANCY: What about the Halloween parade?

LYNN: You *watched.* That was very helpful.
*(Nancy picks up her camera and walks away from Lynn, adjusting her
lens.)*

NANCY: What's with you? That's not fair.

LYNN: *Fair?* I wind up doing everything for everyone every day of the week
and *I'm* not fair? There's always some excuse with you.

NANCY: You mean like I'd rather be with my *own* children?

LYNN: Oh and I don't? What we do is for all the kids.

NANCY: *We?* You mean the elite grand order of mothers in charge.

LYNN: Somebody has to. Forget it. I didn't mean to make it into a big
thing.

NANCY: It's too late, you made it into a big thing. What about helping
out at the nurse's office. What about that?

LYNN: You did it once. Congratulations.

NANCY: Well, maybe if you were home more, your kids wouldn't be wandering around so . . .

LYNN: So *what?* Go on. Going on a class trip doesn't mean you've sold your soul to the devil, you know.

NANCY: Maybe not to you. Besides, maybe I'm shy.

LYNN: You? Shy? Ha. That's your lamest excuse yet. You modeled, for heavens sake.

NANCY: You can be shy and still have your picture taken.

LYNN: Why do you think you're dealing with anything more than the rest of us? Yeah, it's lonely and isolated, but it might be a heck of a lot easier if you joined in.

NANCY: I don't understand why everyone thinks becoming a mother means you become a different person. When I was a kid I never could just walk onto a playground and start talking with the other kids. It took me forever. Now I'm supposed to walk onto a playground, waving and smiling like Miss Extrovert, joining right in with all the chitchat. It's very hard for me. And, believe me, I know this is totally irrelevant to anything, but I *am* trying to make *some* progress with my work.

LYNN: What work?

NANCY: My . . . you know . . . photography.

LYNN: Don't take this the wrong way, Nancy, but I swear to God, I have never seen one picture you've taken, not one.

(Nancy looks at Lynn about to answer, but decides against it.)

NANCY: Look, I'm not interested in class trips or trips of any kind, OK? If you want to knock yourself out with that "stuff," great, do it, but, please, leave me out of it.

LYNN: I knock myself out with that "stuff" because I'm doing something good for the kids and you know what really gets me? Not the work, not the kids, but having other *parents* look down their nose at me like I'm some no-brain volunteer who's not smart enough to be doing something else. I *choose* to do this — I left a great job, a great job! And you know why? Because I like having my kids light up like the Fourth of July when they see me in the school. And I like to be there at that unpredictable moment when one of their most private

thoughts is presented to me like a gift. It's what I want to do and I
wouldn't trade it for anything.

NANCY: You got it wrong, Lynn, nobody looks down on you. They're intimidated by you. *I'm* intimidated by you. But I . . . I *admire* you,
don't you know that? It's just . . . *(She sighs.)* You know why you don't
see any pictures? *(Nancy empties her camera bag upside down and rolls
of undeveloped film fall on the ground.)* I never develop them.

LYNN: Why not?

NANCY: I say it's the kids' fault. That I don't have time. I guess that's par-
tially true, but . . . it's more than that . . . there's something else . . .

LYNN: What? Is it what you said before, about killing you. *What's* killing
you?

NANCY: I keep thinking I'm missing out on something. I used to have this
ecstasy about life that would make me feel so alive. And now . . .

LYNN: Now what Nancy? What?

NANCY: Oh Lynn. In the past six months, there was both Mary and my
sister-in-law. Did you know that right here, on this bench, Mary sat
next to me one Sunday afternoon just a year ago. It was a game that
very few of us showed up for — she looked around, searching for
people, and then she said, with such anger in her voice that she was
shaking, "Where is everybody? What could they be doing that's so
much more important than watching their children play?" I was al-
lowed for a few moments to look through the eyes of a woman who
was seeing life as clearly as you can see it — with a pure and unob-
structed vision. And her words hit me. Profoundly. Where *was* everybody? She knew that with what time she had left all she wanted to
do was look at her children.

LYNN: That was Mary.

(Lynn wipes her eyes. Nancy puts her arm around Lynn.)

NANCY: And then, not more than a couple of months after that, my
sister-in-law made that rare visit to our house. I told you about her —
she had breast cancer.

LYNN: Joanne, right?

NANCY: Yeah, Joanne. She said to me, how are you, and I started talking
about the kids and she said, no, no, *you,* how are *you,* are you going
back to work, are you really going to become a photographer, and

before I could answer she begins to cry and says she wished she had worked at something that was just hers, that belonged to her. That she had actually written the book that she always talked about, but never took the time to do. She had two wonderful boys, but this is what she wanted to talk about. So, you see — children, work, there's always going to be some regret, so I keep thinking if I could just find out what mine will be, maybe I could do something about it. Whatever it is, I think if I don't do something soon, it's going to be too late. The only thing I know for sure is . . . my kids . . . they mean everything to me, so, see? What am I talking about? . . .

LYNN: Maybe . . . *(Shrugs and pats Nancy gently.)* Who wakes up thinking they're going to get hit in the head with a soccer ball?

THE STORY
Tracey Scott Wilson

Dramatic
Yvonne, twenties; Latisha, teens. Both women are black

> *Yvonne is an ambitious newspaper reporter, investigating the murder of a white man in a black neighborhood. Latisha has been the source for her stories about a girl gang who, Latisha claims, killed the man. Here, Latisha reveals that it's all been made up. Lights up on Yvonne trying to pray.*

YVONNE: Our father who art in heaven . . . hallowed be thy name . . . thy kingdom . . . hallowed be . . . Damn.
(Back to prayer.)
YVONNE: *(Continued.)* Our father who . . . haven't done this in a while, not since my . . . I'm just trying to understand why she . . . not really sure how to do this anymore . . . what am I going to . . . I'm . . . I . . . Oh, Lordy, Lordy, Lordy . . . *(Mock slave voice.) (Pause.)* She laughed at me.
(Lights up on Yvonne.)
LATISHA: Listen, I have to tell you something. I didn't mean for things to get this fucked up. First off, my name is not Latisha, and I'm really, really sorry.
YVONNE: Sorry about what?
LATISHA: I'm not . . . I'm not in a gang. *(Pause.)* And I don't know about any murder. . . .
YVONNE: What? What the fuck are you talking about?
LATISHA: I was just playing with you. I was just playing.
YVONNE: Playing?! Are you kidding me? Playing?!
LATISHA: You know I just . . . I go to boarding school and they are fascinated by a ghetto girl like me. Fascinated. How do you get your hair like that? Have you ever seen anybody murdered? I get so sick of it. So, you know, I just make up shit to pass the time. I tell them I'm

in a gang, and my mother is on crack. They think I'm supposed to be like that so I just . . . My mother is a librarian. I barely leave the house when I come home from school.

(Seeing Yvonne's expression.)

LATISHA: *(Continued.)* Are you . . . Are you alright?

YVONNE: Why would you do this to me? Why would you? I told you about my sister, my life. I encouraged you. I helped you.

LATISHA: You helped me? No . . . I . . . See . . . I . . . *(Pause.)* Listen, I'm sorry. I'm . . . *Sono molto spiacente. (Pause.)* I tell you it's hard keeping it real sometimes. *(Pause.)* I don't know . . . *(Pause.)* When I saw you that day I wondered if it would work on one of us. I mean, I could tell you were different. Not really one of us. Like me kinda. Just the way you . . . I don't know. *(Pause.)* I look around my neighborhood and I wish I could move. Everybody acts so stupid. But they're not stupid. They just act stupid. You know Franz Fanon says the oppressed are taught to believe the worst about themselves. So I just wanted to see. I spoke Italian and German to you and you still believed I was in a gang. *(Pause.)* Just like the people at school. *(Pause.)* Just like them. *(Pause.)* So, you need to tell the police that . . .

YVONNE: I'm not retracting my story.

LATISHA: You have to. There are no AOBs. There are no AOBs. I'm calling the paper and telling the truth.

YVONNE: You call the paper and I will tell the police that you killed Tim Dunn. You already told people at your school that you are in a gang. No one will believe you. You fucking brat. This is my career. I will hurt you. I will.

LATISHA: This is crazy.

YVONNE: You laughed at me. Forget that Franz Fanon bullshit, only a stupid-ass Oreo like me would fall for such a ridiculous story, right? You think you are the only one who has something to prove. It never ends, honey. It never ends.

LATISHA: I'm telling . . .

YVONNE: You think anyone will take your word over mine? They won't because keeping it real wanna-be-gangster niggers like you make all black folks look guilty of something.

LATISHA: I'll . . . I'll jack you up for real . . . I'll . . .

(Yvonne laughs at her.)

LATISHA: I'll get somebody to . . . to . . . *(Pause.)* Please . . . please . . . I just . . . I was just playing!

YVONNE: You think it's funny all the white kids at school think you're in a gang? You think it's funny to be ignorant and crude?

(Latisha runs away.)

YVONNE: *(Continued.)* You want to keep keeping it for real now? You want to keep *(Pause to herself.)* keeping it . . . *(Pause.)* Just . . . please, please help me.

AFTER ASHLEY. ©2004 by Gina Gionfriddo. Reprinted by permission of the author. The entire text has been published by Smith and Kraus, Inc. in *Humana Festival 2004: The Complete Plays*. For performance rights, contact the author's agent: Michael Cardonick, Creative Artists Agency, 162 Fifth Ave., 6th Fl., New York, NY 10010. 212-277-9000.

BIRDY. ©2003 by Naomi Wallace. Reprinted by permission of The Rod Hall Agency Ltd., 3 Charlotte Mews, London W1T 4DZ, England. The entire text has been published in an acting edition by Broadway Play Publishing, 56 E 81 St., New York, NY 10028-0202, which also handles performance rights.

CHECK, PLEASE. ©2003 by Jonathan Rand. Reprinted by permission of Playscripts, Inc., which has published the entire text in an acting edition and which also handles performance rights. Contact info: www.Playscripts.com (Web site); info@playscripts.com (e-mail); 866-NEW-PLAY (telephone). Address: Box 237070, New York, NY 10023.

THE COMING WORLD. ©2003 by Christopher Shinn. Reprinted By permission of John Buzzetti, The Gersh Agency, 41 Madison Avenue, 33rd floor, New York, NY 10010. CAUTION: Professionals and amateurs are hereby warned that *The Coming World* is subject to a royalty. It is fully protected under the copyright laws of the United States of America, and of all countries covered by the International Copyright Union (including the Dominion of Canada and the rest of the British Commonwealth), and of all countries covered by the Pan-American Copyright Convention and the Universal Copyright Convention, and of all countries with which the United States has reciprocal copyright relations. All rights, including professional, amateur, motion picture, recitation, lecturing, public reading, radio broadcasting, television, video or sound taping, all other forms of mechanical or electronic reproduction, such as information storage and retrieval systems and photocopying, and the rights of translation into foreign languages, are strictly reserved. Particular emphasis is laid upon the question of readings, permission for which must be secured from the author's agent in writing. The stage performance rights in *The Coming World* (other than first class rights) are controlled exclusively by Dramatists Play Service, Inc., 440 Park Avenue South, New York, NY 10016. No professional or nonprofessional performance of the play (excluding the first class professional performance) may be given without obtaining in advance the written permission of Dramatists Play Service, Inc., and paying the requisite fee. Inquiries concerning all other rights should be addressed to The Gersh Agency, 41 Madison Avenue, 33rd floor, New York, NY 10010. Attn: John Buzzetti.

THE DAZZLE. ©2003 by Richard Greenberg. Reprinted by permission of Far-

222